Flying in Congested Airspace:
A Private Pilot's Guide

TAB
PRACTICAL
FLYING SERIES

No. 2446
$24.95

Flying in Congested Airspace:
A Private Pilot's Guide

Kevin Garrison

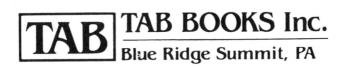
TAB BOOKS Inc.

Blue Ridge Summit, PA

FIRST EDITION
FIRST PRINTING

Copyright © 1989 by **TAB BOOKS Inc.**
Printed in the United States of America

Reproduction or publication of the content in any manner, without express permission
of the publisher, is prohibited. The publisher takes no responsibility for the use of any
of the materials or methods described in this book, or for the products thereof.

Library of Congress Cataloging in Publication Data

Garrison, Kevin.
    Flying in congested air space : a private pilot's guide / by Kevin
Garrison.
        p. cm.
    ISBN 0-8306-9446-3   ISBN 0-8306-2446-5 (pbk.)
    1. Air traffic control—United States. 2. Private flying—United
States
TL725.3.T7G36 1989
629.132′5217—dc20   89-20131
                                                     CIP

TAB BOOKS Inc. offers software for sale. For information and a catalog, please contact
TAB Software Department, Blue Ridge Summit, PA 17294-0850.

Questions regarding the content of this book should be addressed to:

    Reader Inquiry Branch
    TAB BOOKS Inc.
    Blue Ridge Summit, PA 17294-0214

Acquisitions Editor: Jeff Worsinger
Production: Katherine Brown
Series Design: Jaclyn B. Saunders

Contents

Introduction

Technology has certainly made flying safer and quite a bit more predictable. However, technology has also made operating in America's airspace much, much more complicated.

Radar, transponders, and other advances in the science of tracking and controlling the movement of aircraft have made possible today's air traffic control system. It has grown enough to allow the air transportation system of the United States to blossom into the best, most efficient in the world.

It is also true in this country that just about any properly trained citizen-pilot has access to even the busiest, most crowded airports.

A problem arises when pilots that aren't accustomed to operating in the much different, more regimented airspace, attempt to fly in or out of these congested areas. Many feel their way through this airspace and consider themselves lucky when they successfully get in and get out without a problem.

As with most problems in flying, this lack of knowledge can be remedied. With the proper information, any pilot in the United States should be able to land at O'Hare as easily as their home field.

This book is intended for pilots at all levels, including student pilots, that want to learn more about controlled and congested airspace.

Hopefully, the book contains enough information to be a source book for learning the "system" and how to operate in it and remain legal. Also, the book should be a good review for the old hand at flying that might need a refresher from time to time.

This book is not the final authority for all questions regarding legality and safety. Consult FAA publications for the final up-to-date word on regulations and current practices.

1
Introduction
to Survival

"CESSNA ONE-SEVEN ALPHA, TRAFFIC TEN O'CLOCK AND FIVE miles, opposite direction, indicating six thousand five hundred, additional traffic one o'clock three miles, IFR five thousand."

How many times have you gone through the same scenario, even in relatively uncrowded skies?

There is probably nothing more frustrating, frightening and confusing for today's general aviation pilot than flying in areas of the United States where aircraft crowd the skies.

Many pilots lack the skill, knowledge, experience, and confidence to operate in ARSAs, TCAs and high density airports like Denver or Los Angeles. However, it is a fact of life that they must, at least part of the time, face and master large airports. Unfortunately, many pilots are afraid to traverse this airspace and therefore don't realize the potential of their aircraft as a form of easy, fast transportation.

Like most fears, this one is due to a lack of timely, easy-to understand information; this book proposes to provide that information, plus the knowledge and tools necessary for survival in one of the fastest growing problem areas of aviation today: *flying in congested airspace.*

The world of flying has certainly changed in the past 50 years. It was not that long ago that seeing an aircraft of any type was cause for the entire town to quit whatever it was doing and run outside to see the flying

Flying safely in today's airspace hinges on a pilot's skill, knowledge, and experience.

machine overhead. The pilots were heros and those who survived flying for more than a few years were legends.

It is hard to imagine a period of time in which any successful flight was met with wine and celebration. Today every flight is expected, at least by the public, to be conducted safely and the outcome is always assumed to be safe, ordinary, and perhaps even dull.

Days of the rare appearance of an aircraft in the skies are over for most of the United States and the world. More than 207,000 general aviation aircraft in 1987 had to share the skies with over 4,400 airliners and in many cases try to operate in the same airspace with them.

Some of the places you can expect to mix it up with the "big guys" would include cities like Chicago which recorded over 768,000 aircraft movements in 1987. That works out to 2,104 movements a day, 87.6 an hour, and 1.46 a minute. These figures for Chicago are only for the main airport, O'Hare, and don't include other airports in the area like Pal Waulkee, Lakefront, and Glenview Naval Air Station that share the airspace within a 30-mile radius of O'Hare.

Chicago is an obvious choice when you want to spout impressive numbers about crowded skies because it is the busiest airport in the country, however many other places are not considered "congested airspace" but fit the bill nicely.

How about Santa Ana Airport in California with over a half a million aircraft movements a year? Or Denver's Stapleton with over 502,000 movements?

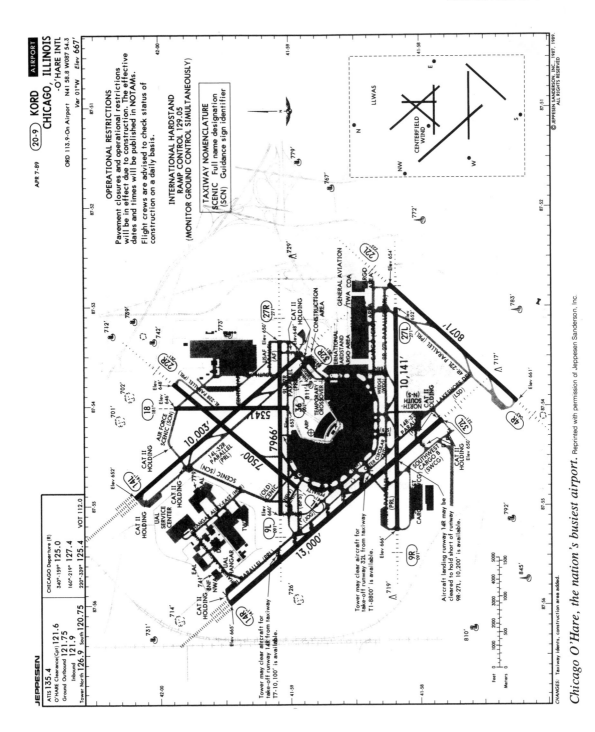

Chicago O'Hare, the nation's busiest airport. Reprinted with permission of Jeppesen Sanderson, Inc.

3

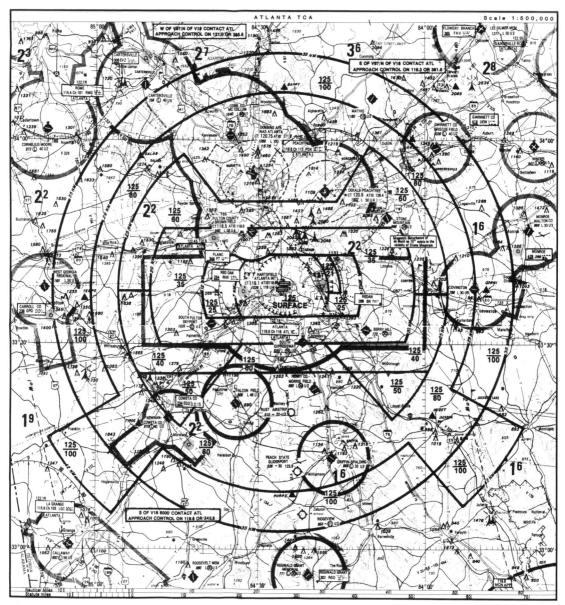

There are many "small airports" in a TCA like Atlanta's.

CONGESTED OR CROWDED?

Unfortunately for today's pilots, there is very little doubt that at least part of their flying is in what most would consider "congested" or "crowded" airspace. The days of climbing into the Cub for a quiet flight in empty skies is over for most of us. This is true for two reasons: demographics and aircraft utilization.

The point about demographics is simple but is so obvious that many people miss it when they lament about how the good old days of aviation seem to be over.

Most of the United States' population lives in, near or around large cities. I realize that many people don't actually live inside large cities like Atlanta, but how many pilots live close and fly their aircraft within a 35 nautical mile radius of Hartsfield International Airport? That mileage figure is the outside border of the Atlanta Group I Terminal Control Area.

Inside the TCA circle around Atlanta are the small towns of Newnan, Covington, Peachtree City, and Stone Mountain, just to name a few.

Even flight lines out in the quiet country are often located near a major airport like O'Hare.

Although each town in the Atlanta area has an airport of different size and complexity, each pilot flying in or out of these airports must deal with having one of the most crowded and busy airports in the country right next door.

Even people living far outside of these large TCA cities must deal with them. A pilot in Albany, Georgia, who wants to fly to Chattanooga or Knoxville has to handle the fact that the Atlanta TCA is right in his way as he plans the course.

The second reason that dealing with crowded skies is just about every pilot's business today is the way that many people use an aircraft.

In the beginning of aviation—when just getting into the air was a novelty and a thrill—little thought was given to "justifying" owning and operating an airplane beyond the fact that it was fun and exciting.

Today, in addition to being fun and exciting, aircraft are used for transportation, as well as many other business and service functions. For many people it is just not good enough to make touch and goes at the local grass strip, they *must* get to that meeting in Charleston tomorrow morning. In other words, as more and more people use an aircraft for transportation and other tasks done—such as forestry flying, banner towing, air ambulance, and national defense, just to name a few—the skies naturally became more crowded and flying became more complex.

It's a tribute to this country, in a way, that we have this problem of crowded skies; if the opposite was true, this country would be in deep trouble. It is still possible for any suitably rated pilot to fly into any civilian field as long as he follows the rules.

Although most of the time I wouldn't recommend that a low-time private pilot with the ink still wet on his ticket climb into a Cessna 152 and fly into JFK in marginal weather, it is perfectly within his rights to do just that.

Many pilots argue that the airways and skies of America are overregulated and too many rules govern their "rights" when it comes to flying. This book will not attempt to get a handle on either side's argument in that matter. While organizations and bureaucracies like the Federal Aviation Administration (FAA), Air Line Pilots Association (ALPA), Aircraft Owners and Pilots Association (AOPA), National Transportation Safety Board (NTSB) and Congress wrestle with the problems of what is right, fair, and best for the economy and defense posture of the United States, you and I are left with the really big problem: How do I deal with the airspace system the way it is and manage to survive while still utilizing my aircraft and enjoying my flying?

That is the purpose of this guide to flying in congested airspace. We will leave the politicking to the politicians and try to get a handle on how to safely fly in today's environment.

As a pilot with a major airline, I usually fly about 80 hours a month in and out of the airspace discussed in this book. Practically everything necessary to cope with congested airspace will be included in this book.

COMPLEX AIRSPACE

Most pilots have some grasp on the rudiments of flying through complex airspace but sometimes it doesn't make much sense; confusion can cause unsafe flying. Any unsafe flying, even caused by honest confusion, is not good for survival.

Let's begin safe flight into congested airspace.

To understand the ATC system today and tomorrow, we must first understand its past. Because the operation of an aircraft in congested airspace is directed, controlled, and influenced by air traffic control (ATC), an understanding of its background and method is necessary.

I shall dissect the entire airspace system bit by bit and then put it back together: a rundown of controlled and uncontrolled airspace, where it is and requirements for separation of VFR and IFR; the TRSA, ARSA, and TCA and how to operate into and out of airports like Chicago O'Hare and Atlanta Hartsfield; review the pertinent FARs and include a glossary of terms, official and slang.

Different ways to handle congested airspace depend on whether you operate VFR or IFR, therefore I shall review procedures for VFR and IFR operations in a Group I TCA.

Finally, I shall discuss things that the FAA, CFI and mother probably never discussed about operating in this environment. Tips and techniques from the real world will be included for an extra edge.

One point that regulation-oriented books fail to see is obvious: it is very possible to be very legal and also be very unsafe while operating in the real world. When talking about safety, whether in a jungle or in the air around Los Angeles International, *common sense* is the most important ingredient to longevity.

2
A Short History of Air Traffic Control

THE SEPARATION AND CONTROL OF AIR TRAFFIC HAS BEEN A PROBLEM ever since the very first flyers took to the skies in the early 1900s. While the main conern of the first pilots was avoiding a collision with the ground and trees, there was concern at the very first airshows and circuses that the aircraft might run into each other. Pilots who have attended a large fly-in like Oshkosh can appreciate the trouble early pioneers endured.

Official concern for collision avoidance began just after World War I, when the International Committee on Air Navigation was formed. Few people remember this committee, but their aviation lives are affected everyday by the actions the group took: which side the aircraft red and green navigation lights would be on, right of way rules, and a standardized system of ground control—using flares and red or green lights—was instituted. In the years that followed many countries including the United States adopted the new rules of airmanship.

Aviation boomed briefly after WWI with experienced and unemployed military airmen and cheap, inexpensive, and easily available war surplus aircraft. Most of this boom was expressed in stunt flying and airshows of all types, including flying circuses, some returning airmen were more interested in establishing airmail and, later, passenger service. For the most part, though, the flying game was perceived as one of freedom and high adventure for the participant.

This changed somewhat in the late 1920s. An important clue to the future of aviation worldwide was a meeting in Paris, France, that was known as the "Convention of Paris." The convention laid down rules for European air traffic.

Rules similar to those in Europe were adopted by the United States in 1928 shortly after the Havana Air Convention. The rules were resented by many people who were concerned with the "freedom of the skies," but they did set a legal precedent that would be important later. The new rules were very similar to the laws regulating other forms of transportation and in adopting them the nations clearly claimed sovereignty over the airspace above their territory: air rights.

The first actual scheduled airline flight took place in 1914: a Benoist Type XIV flying boat across Tampa Bay from St. Petersburg to Tampa. Official government concern about the safety and separation of air traffic surfaced in May 1918 with the first airmail route between Washington, Philadelphia, and New York. Routes from New York to Cleveland and Chicago soon followed.

Coast-to-coast airmail service began in 1921 and with it the airline industry that we know today.

A much larger problem than collision for the early airliners was navigation, especially at night and in poor weather conditions. Prior to the pioneering work that Jimmy Doolittle did in blind flying in the late 1920s, all flying, including airmail, was done under visual conditions.

One attempt to help the airmail pilot navigate at night was in 1921 when Jack Knight became famous for flying guided by bonfires set by farmers along his route.

Rotating beacons were the next logical step for nighttime air navigation. The 72 mile stretch from Columbus to Dayton, Ohio, was equipped with a series of rotating beacons. Army pilots made over 25 successful runs using these navaids. In addition to the beacons , field floodlights and flashing markers were set along the course. The deHavilland DH-4Bs were outfitted with landing lights and two parachute flares.

This system of flares, lights, and beacons was adopted nationwide and was in place by late 1927. More than 2,000 miles of lighted airways existed in the United States by the end of that year and they stretched from coast-to-coast.

No light, beacon, or flare in the world could solve the problem the early pilots frequently ran into when trying to keep a schedule: bad weather. Then as now, weather was a very large problem.

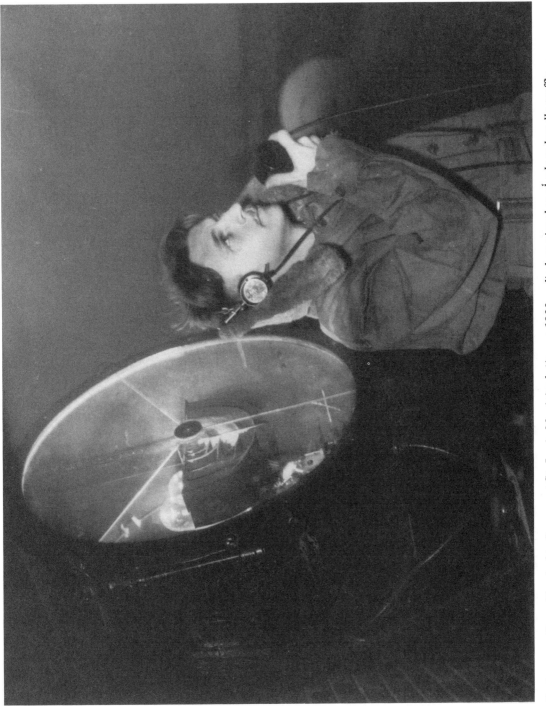

Early controllers, like Archie League at St. Louis Municipal Airport 1933, relied on visual methods to handle traffic. FAA

With use of the new artificial horizon and directional gyro, and improvements made to the sensitive altimeter, Jimmy Doolittle changed the aviation world by conducting the first completely blind flight in September 1929.

Advances in navigation, combined with improvements to the design and reliability of aircraft of the day, gradually led to the problem of air traffic. Establishment of airline passenger service in 1927, plus the advent of the first truly modern airliners—the Boeing 247 and the DC-2—ushered in a new way of travel and a new problem was born.

The nation's airways connected the large cities and in so doing concentrated air traffic over the areas with highest populations. No one wanted to think what would happen if two aircraft collided over Manhattan, but they had to admit that the possibility existed.

Early attempts at air traffic control began at busier airports at large cities. Signals employed by the ancient controllers were visual and useless in low visibility conditions and at night.

To control the traffic pattern, a person placed himself in a prominent place on the field where the pilots had a good chance of seeing him and used two flags to signal approaching aircraft: a checkered or green flag to approve landing, a solid red flag to hold or go-around. Other later refinements were the light-gun signals (still in use) and the 1930s, radio. The first experimental radios were used in Cleveland in 1930. Other radios were installed at other locations afterward, using low-powered transmitters. These methods were used mainly to control takeoffs and the pilots were under no real compunction to always follow the instructions.

Fear of collision became so compelling in 1935 that American, United, TWA, and Eastern Airlines set up a corporation and established an airway traffic control unit in the Newark Airport terminal building. This unit was to control the flow of traffic through the very busy New York area. The unit was deemed a success and others were set up in Cleveland and Chicago.

Although these facilities were successful they solved only a tiny fraction of the air traffic problem. Private aircraft as well as military aircraft did not have to take part in the control program because no rules told them to do so. In addition, the centers only controlled airliners in and out of the major terminals, had absolutely no direct communication with them and, when push came to shove, had no real authority over them.

The federal government took control of these airway traffic control centers in 1936 and began its long journey into directing air traffic in the United States. Local airport towers remained private.

Controllers had to communicate with the pilots in a round-about fashion. When issuing clearances or instructions, controllers first had to contact the airline company. The airline dispatcher would then pass the information along to the pilot in the air, either through direct radio contact, or by relaying the message through Department of Commerce radio operators.

An early airport tower and local controller.

Earl Ward (left) was responsible for organizing airline traffic centers in 1935. Here, at the Newark Center, with Dick Aldsworth, he plots aircraft movement over New Jersey in 1937. FAA

All separation of aircraft was accomplished by dead reckoning. Pilots would call in position reports at regular intervals over required locations, giving their estimate for the next fix, much as IFR pilots do today in non-radar environments. The controller would separate aircraft by use of estimates and different altitudes. Controller tools included a blackboard for flight progress, a map table, and a teletype machine or telephone to relay clearances to the pilot.

It should be noted that traffic control was only within established airways well into the late 1950s. If a flight was off the airways it was on its own and completely out of controlled airspace. This not only meant that a pilot could take any route, but that VFR separation and visibility minimums that are so familiar today did not exist. If a pilot could fly on instruments he was perfectly legal to do so without a clearance of any kind. As a matter of fact, it can still be done today inside what is left of uncontrolled airspace in this country, usually below either 1,200 or 800 feet AGL.

By the eve of United States participation in World War II, 15 full-time Air Route Traffic Control Centers (ARTCCs) operated on a 24-hour basis, by the end of the war 19 centers (today there are 20) and most local control towers were operated by the Civil Aeronautics Administration. Things remained like that until the end of WWII brought its tremendous changes in the system and the way people thought about air travel and airplanes.

AFTER WORLD WAR II

The end of the war brought new technology and ideas into the realm of air traffic control. The most obvious of course was radar and the institution of direct radio communication between controllers and pilots. One of the underlying and less obvious ingredients to post-war controlling was the war experience brought home by Americans. For example, American bomb raid planners had to accommodate flight of hundreds of aircraft at a single moment. Another factor rarely considered is that the pilots returning from the war to become corporate and airline pilots were accustomed to government control while in the air.

Even with introduction of these new tools, the system was slow to adopt them. It was late 1949 when the first two-way radio communications were instituted at Chicago Center. It was a full six years before this capability was extended to other centers.

After the war the country was uncomfortable about spending large sums of money for an upgraded air traffic control system. Although the

Truman administration had adopted a plan for modernization in 1949, the Korean War and a general public disinterest slowed funding. The CAA's staffing level in 1955 was identical to 1947, even though passenger traffic on the airlines had doubled since 1949.

A large part of the problem in post-war America was a need for long-range radars for separation of air traffic. The administration realized this need but was concerned about cost. Unfortunately, it would take a disaster of epic proportions, which might have been avoided by a modern ATC system, to make the American public demand safer skies.

The midair collision of two airliners over the Grand Canyon in 1956 alerted the American public to pitfalls of the air traffic control system in the United States. As if rubbing salt into the wound, the accident didn't even happen in bad weather or in crowded skies. It happened in the clear above a cloud deck over a vast, uncrowded expanse of airspace.

Both airliners were totally legal, following regulations of the day, and operating in what they thought was a safe fashion. The collision was between two four-engine transports operated by two major airlines with experienced pilots and good safety records.

One was a Trans World Airlines Lockheed Super Constellation carrying 64 passengers and a full crew of six; the second was a United Airlines DC-7 with 53 passengers and a crew of five. Both aircraft were piloted by senior captains and both aircraft were flying to the east coast from Los Angeles.

Initially, Los Angeles Center assigned the TWA Constellation to an altitude of 19,000 feet and the United DC-7 to 21,000 feet. Because of build ups in the Daggett, California area, the TWA Captain requested a climb to 21,000 feet to avoid the clouds. This was denied because of United at 21,000 feet. Positive control airspace didn't exist in 1956, so the TWA crew was well within their rights to request VFR on top and climb to 21,000 feet. They were unaware of the United flight at that altitude and ATC was not required to tell them. Remember, when VFR, traffic separation is the pilot's responsibility. Los Angeles center received the only verbal clue about what was going on: a barely readable transmission from the United flight and only three words, "We are going . . .," could be made out.

No one survived and for the first time, in horrifying detail the American public and the Congress realized just how primitive our ATC system was and how much improvement had to take place.

Because of the public outrage at the condition of the nation's airspace, money for the improvement of air safety was easy to find. In 1958

The Washington ARTCC in 1955 used surplus Navy VG (video generator) "battleship" radars with plastic shrimp boats. Along the walls were plan position indicators, which were radars used to service certain airspace sectors. FAA

Senator Mike Monroney of Oklahoma and 33 cosponsors introduced a bill to create an independent Federal Aviation Agency (FAA) "to provide for the safe and efficient use of the airspace by both civil and military operations and to provide for the regulation and promotion of civil aviation in such a manner as to best foster its development and safety."

The bill was signed into law by President Eisenhower on August 23, 1958, and the FAA was born with two important powers.

> "The control of the use of the country's navigable airspace and the regulation of both civil and military operations within that airspace in the interests of the safety and efficiency of both."

> "The development an operation of a common system of air navigation and air traffic control for both civil and military aviation."

There was one huge surprise in the bill. In a country concerned with checks and balances and the monitoring of those in power, the bill provided that absolutely no one could overrule the FAA administrator on decisions where safety was a factor.

COMPUTER AND RADAR

It was fortunate that the FAA was graced with enough power to regulate air traffic and the coming of the jet age. Shortly after the FAA's official life began, the Boeing 707 took to the skies in scheduled services, followed by many other jet airliners and, later, corporate jet aircraft.

With the introduction of jets into the day-to-day life of the controller came new problems. No longer did the controller and the pilot have the luxury of a 400 knot closure speed with head-on traffic. Now the closure speeds would be in excess of 1,100 knots.

A huge FAA expansion project in 1960 would upgrade and equip "an entirely new complement of air route control centers at 32 locations in the United States." The system installed was a combination of computers and radar much like the semi-automatic ground environment (SAGE) system that the Air Force had been using at its Air Defense Command sites.

Going into the 1970s, traffic congestion problems at the large terminals were addressed by the FAA's program of terminal control areas, which will be discussed in depth in a later chapter.

According to the FAA's figures, cited in an FAA publication, the number of midair collisions and near misses dropped dramatically within months of the TCA system.

The combination of the computer and the radar evolved throughout the 1960s and 1970s from the simple sets that could only detect primary

The mating of the computer and radar made great strides in air traffic control efficiency.

targets and were cluttered with ground and weather returns to advanced presentations that included aircraft ID, speed, and could predict traffic conflicts well in advance of the occurrence.

A major crisis arose on August 3, 1981, when 11,438 controllers, represented by PATCO (Professional Air Traffic Controllers Organization), staged an illegal strike and were subsequently fired by President Reagan.

The wisdom of the strike or even the mass firing of controllers is not pertinent here. An entire book could be written on that subject. It is important to note that for probably the first time the FAA had to face the fact that it had personnel problems that had to be addressed: controller burnout, heavy work loads with little rest, inadequate communication with management, and what controllers considered inadequate pay. Many people would argue that the controller work force still faces many of these problems.

THE FUTURE

It seems that we have an adequate ATC system in the continental United States despite very large holes in coverage Alaska, the Caribbean, and the transoceanic and polar routes. These areas have no radar coverage and still rely on 1930s time-rate-distance calculations and planned separation distances of over 100 miles to keep traffic safe.

According to many observers, the next generation of ATC equipment will come from space in the form of satellite technology. Communications, navigation, and surveillance tasks can be accomplished from earth orbit and would cover the entire globe. Satellite weather communications should also soon become a reality.

WILL THE GENERAL AVIATION PILOT SURVIVE?

No doubt that all the new technology should help the huge airline companies improve safety, but how will new technology help the general aviation pilot?

It is true that in order to operate in TCAs and other special airspace there is a requirement for expensive equipment that excludes many pilots; it has dramatically improved the statistics of air safety—if not actually improving safety—at the larger terminals.

Perhaps it is a false hope, but I believe with the introduction of inexpensive area navigation and satellite communications, the cost of these ATC "safety equipment" requirements will continually drop and become

Cessna Aircraft Company

Will the general aviation pilot retain a place in the future of America's air traffic control system?

available to just about anyone who operates an airplane in the United States.

After all, the only way to have a genuinely safe system of air traffic control is to make it available and affordable to all the users.

We shall see.

3
America's Airspace from the Ground Up

IN ORDER TO BEST EXPLAIN THE NATIONAL AIRSPACE SYSTEM OF THE United States, it would be a good idea to explain *controlled* and *uncontrolled* airspace. The subject of controlled airspace is a little confusing because "controlled" in the case of airspace means different things to different people at different times. The airspace above Chicago's O'Hare is controlled like the airspace above Shreveport, Louisiana, but what you can and cannot do in the respective airspace is vastly different. Survival in congested airspace depends upon knowing the "rules of the jungle." The government's official definition of controlled airspace and a guided tour of the nation's airspace system: both controlled and uncontrolled, from the ground up to the edge of space.

CONTROLLED AIRSPACE

The FAA's definition of controlled airspace seems to be a vague description of a complex subject. It really is vague because the subject is so complex. Let's look at the FAA's definition and then paraphrase it to make it a little more understandable to non-lawyers.

Controlled airspace is designated as a continental control area, control area, control zone, terminal control area, transition area, or positive control area, *within which some or all aircraft may be subject to air traffic control.*

Throughout the remainder of the definition FAA explains what they mean by a control zone, transition area, and so on. The definition, although short and sweet raises more questions than it answers. What do they mean by "all or some aircraft may be subject to air traffic control?"

The International Civil Aviation Organization (ICAO) definition of controlled airspace makes a little more sense, is shorter, and is more to the point:

(ICAO) Controlled Airspace: Airspace of defined dimensions within which air traffic control service is provided to controlled flights.

For our purposes, a combination and slight alteration of both definitions is a good idea because controlled airspace means vastly different things to different operators, depending on how they intend to utilize it. Many VFR pilots flying on a nice day at 3,500 ft. over the countryside would vehemently say that they weren't flying in controlled airspace (even though they were) because no one was "controlling" them.

A control zone, means something quite different to a 727 captain operating on an IFR clearance than it means to a Cessna 172 driver trying to maintain legal VFR and still operate in that airspace. Although they are both operating in the same airspace and trying to land at the same airport, different rules apply to these pilots and how they conduct their flight.

Basically, controlled airspace of all types, from TCA group I to local *airport traffic control areas* exist for two simple reasons (in order):

1. To exclude certain aircraft from that airspace for reasons of either poor weather or high traffic conditions for the purpose of providing the aircraft that do operate in that airspace separation and traffic avoidance.

   This part of the definition would especially include the TCA and ARSA, which will be covered in depth in later chapters. Even when the weather is crystal clear, many aircraft are excluded from this airspace because of equipment, pilot experience, and licensing requirements. A non-radio Aeronca Champ flown by a student pilot would not be welcome in the traffic pattern at Atlanta's Hartsfield, mixing it up with the L-1011s.

2. The second reason controlled airspace exists is to provide a framework in which other FARs are effective. Many people don't realize that most of the VFR separation from clouds and visibility requirements are for *controlled airspace only*. Same thing applies for IFR pilots. Did you know that it is legal in this country to

operate an aircraft in the clouds, IFR, without a clearance in uncontrolled airspace? Yep, you can. All you need is an instrument rating and an aircraft capable of flying through the clouds.

The catch, of course, is that the uncontrolled airspace you'd be flying through would be so low and close to the ground, trees, buildings, and power lines that under most circumstances you'd have to be crazy to try it, plus all the instrument approaches in the country are protected by controlled airspace and are legally unavailable in low weather unless you're on an IFR flight plan and a clearance.

Of course, you probably have already figured out that there is more than one kind of "controlled airspace." The controlled airspace just above a transition area is much different from the controlled airspace above Flight Level 180.

A transition area can have a combination of VFR and IFR aircraft operating at the same time. Above 18,000 feet positive control is in effect and you can't operate without an IFR clearance, certain required equipment, and of course the appropriate instrument rating.

CONTROLLED AIRSPACE AND THE VFR PILOT

The VFR pilot flying in controlled airspace is concerned about maintaining basic VFR weather minimums. Highly restrictive visibility and cloud separation requirements exist when flying through controlled airspace than when operating outside the controlled airspace system. For example, in controlled airspace below 10,000 ft. MSL, at least three miles visibility is required to operate a flight. This way, on scuzzy, low visibility days when you want to fly out of a controlled airport you are excluded from the airspace if the visibility is below three. Why? To protect IFR flights operating in the area.

If you are at an uncontrolled airport that is outside other controlled airspace restrictions (transition areas, control zones, etc.), you could fly with one mile visibility and remain clear of the clouds. The separation and visibility rules in Part 91.105 should be familiar to every private pilot in the United States. More separation and more visibility are required at higher altitudes to stay legal. The logic behind this is that the higher altitudes contain faster aircraft, such as jets, and reaction time to traffic would be much shorter than at the lower altitudes with slower aircraft.

Remember, below 10,000 ft. MSL all traffic is limited to 250 kias (knots indicted airspeed), above 10,000, aircraft can go as fast as able. In airliners like the DC-9 and 727 pilots gently push over at ten thousand and

VFR separation minimums.

ALTITUDE	UNCONTROLLED AIRSPACE		CONTROLLED AIRSPACE	
	FLIGHT VISIBILITY	DISTANCE FROM CLOUDS	**FLIGHT VISIBILITY	**DISTANCE FROM CLOUDS
1,200' or less above the surface, regardless of MSL altitude.	*1 statute mile	Clear of clouds	3 statute miles	500' below 1,000' above 2,000' horizontal
More than 1,200' above the surface, but less than 10,000' MSL.	1 statute mile	500' below 1,000' above 2,000' horizontal	3 statute miles	500' below 1,000' above 2,000' horizontal
More than 1,200' above the surface and at or above 10,000' MSL.	5 statute miles	1,000' below 1,000' above 1 statute mile horizontal	5 statute miles	1,000' below 1,000' above 1 statute mile horizontal

*Helicopters may operate with less than one mile visibility, outside controlled airspace at 1,200 feet or less above the surface, provided they are operated at a speed that allows the pilot adequate opportunity to see any air traffic or obstructions in time to avoid collisions.

**In addition, when operating within a control zone beneath a ceiling, the ceiling must not be less than 1,000 feet. If the pilot intends to land or take off or enter a traffic pattern within a control zone, the ground visibility must be at least three miles at that airport. If ground visibility is not reported at the airport, three miles flight visibility is required. (FAR 91.105)

Aircraft like the Boeing 737 routinely accelerate to 300 knots when above 10,000 feet.

accelerate to 300 knots or more before continuing the climb. If VFR at 10,500 a general aviation pilot would have a lot less time to see and avoid an airliner than when flying at 2,000 where an airliner would probably be slowed to 180 knots, on approach, with landing lights on.

CONTROLLED AIRSPACE AND THE IFR PILOT

It's much simpler for the IFR pilot. Whenever you are operating under an ATC clearance, assume that you are in controlled airspace and afforded the protection of VFR weather minimums that should restrict traffic.

Controllers have absolutely no jusrisdiction over uncontrolled airspace and can't issue a clearance to enter it. Controllers can cancel an IFR flight plan if requested but when a flight exits controlled airspace the pilot is on his own. It should be interesting to note that *no IFR restrictions exist in uncontrolled airspace*.

Can a pilot fly through clouds in uncontrolled airspace without a clearance? Sure, but keep in mind the small amount of uncontrolled airspace, how low to the ground it usually is, and the fact that other pilots who might try this are probably around and protection from them is non-existent. Also, you cannot shoot an instrument approach out of this scenario unless you air-file because all instrument approaches are protected by some form of controlled airspace.

The best way to explain controlled and uncontrolled airspace of the United States and how airspace works is to first clear your mind of all distractions and the many things you "thought" you knew about the subject. Following one major statement about the system will be dozens of exceptions, of course.

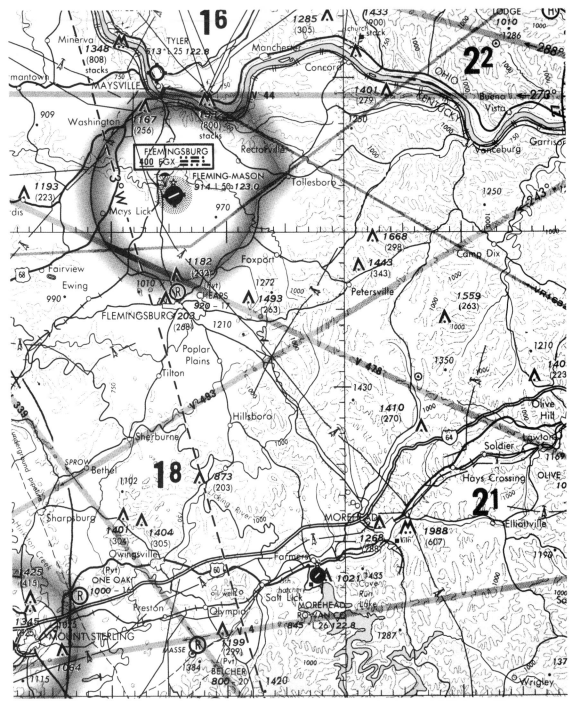

At Morehead Rowan County Airport, the floor of controlled airspace begins at 1,200 feet AGL.

Imagine waiting on the ground at Morehead, Rowan County Airport about to begin a flight. Where does controlled airspace begin here? Controlled airspace begins at exactly 1,200 ft. above the ground. (Major statement.)

An important thing to note is that some controlled airspace is denoted in feet MSL (Mean Sea Level) and other controlled airspace is denoted in AGL (Above Ground Level). The floor of controlled airspace does begin at 1,200 ft. AGL, but in high terrain, such as the Salt Lake City, Utah, area it is not unusual to be at an altitude of 5,000 ft. MSL and still be in uncontrolled airspace.

Most student pilots would be able to tell you where controlled airspace begins above Morehead Airport. Now the important question: What does it mean?

What it means to a VFR pilot is that below 1,200 ft. AGL at this airport, he must maintain clear of clouds with a mile visibility in order to be "legally" VFR. Above 1,200 ft. AGL, the VFR pilot must have 500 below, 1,000 above, 2,000 to the side of any clouds and at least three statute miles visibility.

How do you measure 2,000 ft. to the side of a cloud? Beats me. There is no exact way to estimate distance to the side of a cloud. The visibility rule would have to be an estimate also unless operating near an airport that has a weather observer.

If you're operating an IFR flight out of Morehead, Rowan County, you would not be afforded the protection of the air traffic control (ATC) system, even in bad weather, until you were above 1,200 ft. AGL. If the weather was "500 overcast with one mile visibility" aircraft could legally fly in and out of this airport VFR and ATC would have no control over them and probably couldn't warn you about them.

TRANSITION AREAS

The first and simplest exception to this 1,200 ft. AGL rule is north, northeast of the Morehead, Rowan County Airport found on the Cincinnati sectional that we've been using for an example. It is Fleming-Mason Airport.

Three things can be noticed at first glance. First, there is a little parachute, denoting a jump zone: something important to keep in mind in the area. Second is the fact that there is a nondirectional beacon on the field; this would tend to indicate an NDB instrument approach to this airport. Third, and the most important to this discussion, is the fact that the airport is surrounded by a magenta circle: a transition area.

A transition area means that the floor of controlled airspace is lowered from 1,200 ft. AGL to 700 ft. AGL.

Usually a transition area is placed over an airport or a group of airports that use a navaid such as a nondirectional beacon or VOR to establish a non-precision approach. The main reason for the existence of transition areas is to exclude VFR traffic from the usual base of controlled airspace (1,200 ft. AGL) down to 700 ft. AGL to protect that airspace for aircraft on an IFR clearance that are shooting the approach to that airport.

Most non-precision approaches have minimum descent altitudes (MDAs) of 700-800 ft. AGL. If no transition area existed, it is possible that you could be outbound from the fix, in and out of the clouds with a mile visibility and be face to face with a VFR aircraft that was operating below the floor of controlled airspace. It is also possible, using the same scenario, that you could run into an IFR aircraft flying through the clouds without a clearance below the floor.

While shooting an NDB approach into an airport like Fleming-Mason, remember that the protection afforded by the ATC system ends when you descend below the floor of controlled airspace, in this case, 700 ft. AGL. Below 700 ft., traffic separation and avoidance is the pilot's responsibility.

If six aircraft are in the VFR traffic pattern at Fleming-Mason when at "breakout" it is the pilot's responsibility to avoid them and enter the traffic pattern; the other aircraft have a legal right to be there.

CONTROL ZONES AND AIRPORT TRAFFIC CONTROL AREAS

Lexington, Kentucky, offers the next exception to the 1,200 ft. rule. Surrounding Lexington's Bluegrass Airport on the chart see a dashed line drawn in a circle, roughly five nautical miles around the field. To the northeast of the field, you will see a small "keyhole" shape sticking out.

This, of course, is a control zone. A control zone really means that controlled airspace goes down to the ground and up to the continental control area. The continental control area will be explained later.

Whatever you do, don't confuse a control zone with an airport traffic control area! The airport traffic control area is the five statute mile radius, up to, but not including 3,000 ft. AGL airspace that a control tower controls.

If you're confused about the difference you're not alone. Although most control zones have airports that also have airport traffic control

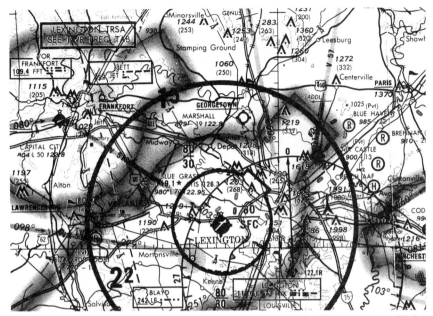

Control zones are another exception to the 1,200-foot rule. The Lexington TRSA inner circle is a control zone.

areas, it is not a requirement. Also, control zones can have more than one airport.

The most important difference between a control zone and an airport traffic control area is what's required of the pilot.

In a control zone a VFR pilot must maintain VFR weather and cloud separation minimums required in controlled airspace. In an airport traffic control area, a pilot is operating with an actual clearance—either VFR or IFR, issued from the tower—and you are illegally in that airspace no matter what the weather without a clearance.

The airport traffic control area is never depicted on a chart. You know a tower exists because either the color of the airport on the VFR chart is blue or the existence of a control tower frequency in the airport data block. In the IFR world, you would know whether or not a tower was in operation at the airport by checking either the *Airport/Facility Directory*, the en route chart, or the airport approach chart.

TERMINAL RADAR PROGRAM

This program isn't actually a part of controlled airspace, but is important because it could save your life. The Terminal Radar Program was started to extend IFR terminal radar services to VFR aircraft.

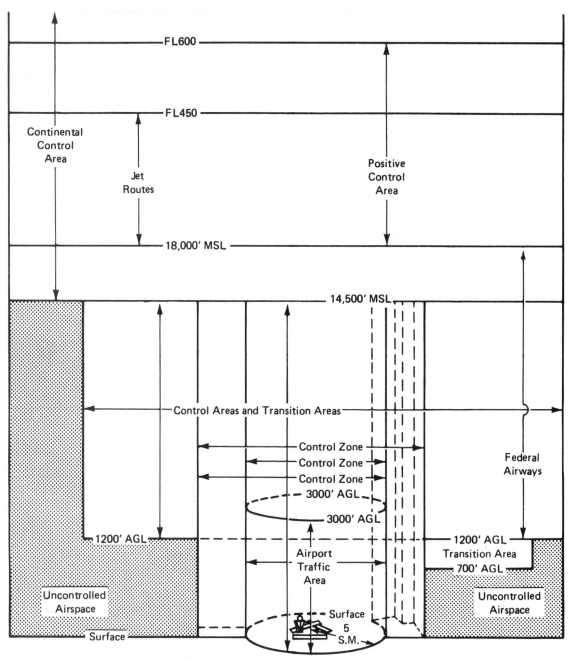

A simple breakdown of the controlled airspace structure in the United States. FAA

Many of us can remember the not too distant past when a VFR pilot requesting radar service from a local approach controller might be turned down because the controller was "too busy" handling IFR traffic. This didn't make much sense because it seemed that keeping VFR and IFR traffic from running into each other would save a lot of paperwork. Officially though, the controllers were right; their job was to separate and sequence IFR traffic. With institution of the Terminal Radar Program the FAA recognized that it would be a good idea to separate everybody.

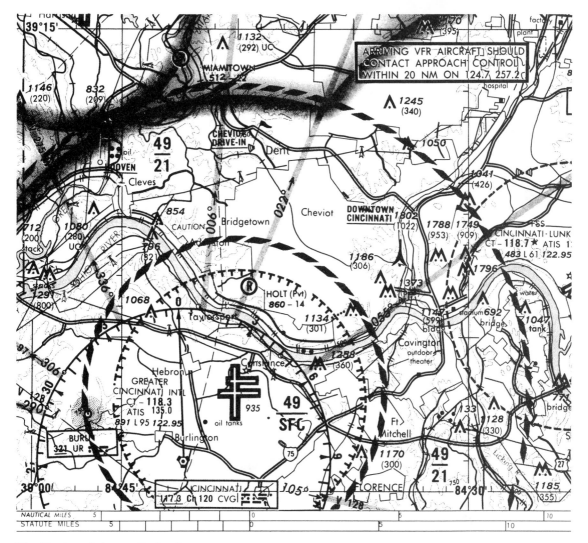

The Cincinnati Airport Radar Service Area.

33

The program is totally voluntary for the VFR pilot and is divided into two parts, Stage Two and Stage Three. Any radar facility is considered a Stage One location. The chapter on ARSAs will further describe radar.

Along V97 to Cincinnati is another form of controlled airspace, the ARSA or Airport Radar Service Area. An ARSA is an area around an airport where radar separation of traffic, VFR and IFR, is mandatory.

An ARSA requires an operating control tower, a radar approach facility, at least 75,000 annual instrument flights at the primary airport, or a combination of 100,000 instrument flight operations a year at primary and secondary airports. If served by airlines, the primary airport in an ARSA must enplane at least 250,000 passengers a year.

On the VFR chart, an ARSA is shown in slashed magenta.

The area of a standard ARSA extends from the surface to 4,000 feet above the ground level of the primary airport for a five nautical mile radius. Five to 10 nautical miles from the primary airport the ARSA runs between 1,200 ft. AGL to 4,000 ft. AGL. Many ARSAs are different due to terrain, other controlled airspace nearby, international boundaries, and other factors.

The only requirement at this date for operating in an ARSA is that you maintain two-way radio communication with the controlling facility. The FAA *does* recommend that you have a transponder but as of now it is not a requirement. Refer to the chapter about ARSAs for better up-to-date information.

TCAs

The last surface controlled airspace is the Terminal Control Area (TCA.)

TCAs are the "upside-down wedding cakes" that place severe restrictions on aircraft operation.

Each TCA surrounds a large, high traffic volume airport and it has been either lauded as the savior of air traffic control or assailed as yet another step in the government's curtailment of our flying freedom. The important fact to keep in mind is that they do exist and must be managed.

While in a TCA, VFR and IFR pilots must have certain equipment on board the aircraft and must follow a clearance from ATC.

A later chapter dedicated solely to survival in a TCA will provide great detail on TCA structure, rules, and how to fly through it.

You don't have to fly a jet to deal with a TCA.

HIGHER

Higher altitudes reveal many more types of controlled and uncontrolled airspace.

Federal Airways

In this case, the best way to explain the federal airways system in the United States would be to quote from the FAA's *Instrument Flying Handbook*:

> Each federal airway is based on a centerline that extends from one navigation aid or intersection to another navigation air (or through several other navigation aids or intersections) specified for that airway. The infinite number of radials transmitted by the VOR permits 360 possible separate airway courses to or from the facility, one for each degree of azimuth. Thus, a given VOR located within approximately 100 miles of several other VORs may be used to establish a number of different airways."

Most federal airways are made up of VOR radials, but some are made specifically for operators with RNAV (area navigation) capability.

The base of an airway is at least 1,200 ft. AGL, the base of controlled airspace. The first layer of federal airways is called "Victor airways" and run from 1,200 ft. AGL up to, but not including 18,000 ft. MSL.

Victor airways are referred to by most airline and corporate jet pilots as the "low altitude structure." While operating in these federally mandated "highways of the sky," a pilot is in controlled airspace, however VFR conditions even the airline pilot or corporate jet jock is vulnerable to the scud-runner or VFR pilot who is lost.

Jet Routes

As we discussed in Chapter 2 the advent of the jet airliner caused ATC many added problems in terms of separating faster jet aircraft from the slower aircraft and improving the survivability of both slow and fast aircraft in the same skies.

The base of the Continental Control Area is 14,500 ft. MSL and the airspace rises infinitely. It is conceivable that the Moon is in the Continental Control Area if the FAA's definition is taken literally because no upper limit is prescribed.

The Continental Control Area is also significant because it is the top of all uncontrolled airspace in the United States. If you're above 14,500 you are definitely in controlled airspace of some kind.

The Continental Control Area is 2,000 ft. *above* the lowest altitude you can operate an aircraft in the United States without a 4096 Mode C transponder. At 12,500 feet, whether in controlled airspace or not, an aircraft must be transponder equipped and it must be operating.

Jet aircraft usually begin cruise segments at or above 18,000 ft. MSL where the advantage of having jet engines comes to the fore. Below 18,000 jets are gas hogs and burn more fuel than a comparable turboprop or piston aircraft. When jets do cruise though, they really cruise. It is not unusual for an average, run of the mill airliner, like the Boeing 727, to fly in cruise at 560 knots, or about .86 the speed of sound.

Obviously in this kind of environment, where aircraft can close on each other head-on at speeds of more than 1,500 miles per hour—almost 13 times the closure speed of two cars head-on at 60 mph—some form of control beyond the "see and be seen" concept, used at the lower, slower levels, is necessary.

Above 18,000 ft. MSL all pilots set barometric altimeters to 29.92 inches of mercury (1013.2 millibars) and enter the realm of the "high altitude structure."

Above 18,000 ft. MSL the altitudes are no longer named after how high they are above sea level, they are called "Flight Levels." In addition to making the altitude easier to understand when spoken over the radio, and sounding trendy, they are called flight levels for the simple reason that unless the altimeter setting on the ground below is exactly 29.92 inches you have no idea how high you are above sea level.

Don't discount the fact that altitudes are easier to understand in flight levels. "Delta 123, climb to and maintain flight level three-one-zero" sounds clearer than "Delta 123 climb and maintain thirty one thousand feet."

Because members of this high altitude "club" travel fast over many different areas with different altimeter settings, it is considered safer for traffic altitude separation to have all altimeters set to this standard. When the altimeter setting at lower levels is less than 29.92 inches, lower flight levels are unusable.

Positive Control Airspace

All altitudes between 18,000 ft. MSL and Flight Level 600 belong in Positive Control Airspace.

Positive control means exactly that —if you want to operate an aircraft legally in the airspace above FL 180 you must be instrument rated and qualified, be flying a properly equipped aircraft and be operating on an IFR clearance. The logic of this rule is pretty simple. At the higher altitudes aircraft routinely cruise at speeds of more than 600 mph for a potential closure speed of more than 1,200 mph. There must be some mandatory protection at these speeds to reduce the risk of midairs.

High altitude, or jet, airways are fewer and farther between but they do have the advantage of long range reception for navigation radios, they are not crowded like low routes and you are under the watchful eye of a controller who is supposed to ensure separation.

The jet route structure runs from the base of Positive Control Airspace up to FL 450. Aircraft above that altitude are primarily military operations.

Above FL 240 an aircraft must also have a usable DME (distance measuring equipment) receiver. Many airliners and military aircraft are equipped with more navigational equipment than listed by the FARs, but you might be surprised to learn that many of them are equipped with the bare minimum required for flight at these altitudes. The standard, stock Boeing 727 used by just about every major airline in the United States is usually equipped with two navcoms, two DMEs a transponder and one ADF! The equipment is reliable and it does the job. Most people who fly aircraft like a Beechcraft Baron and a Piper Malibu might be interested to learn that the DMEs on the 727s don't usually have a ground speed readout. Many airline pilots still use the "time the mileage and divide by six" method to determine approximate ground speed.

Equipment rules for higher altitudes as well as other areas of controlled airspace are changing. On July 1, 1989, an encoding altimeter will be required to fly above 12,500 ft. MSL or within 30 nautical miles of a TCA.

Phase II of this program begins Dec. 30, 1990, when an aircraft will be required to have an encoder flying into or above any ARSA and at other airports to be designated in the future. More will be said about required equipment as we discuss these different sections of airspace separately in later chapters.

Always refer to FARs and AIM for current information.

SPECIAL USE AIRSPACE

Even though this book is dedicated to survival in congested airspace, discussion of different forms of "special use airspace" is wise.

Isn't special use airspace something out in the desert, like bombing ranges? Yes, it is in areas in the "boonies" but also run in crowded areas like TCAs. Numerous restricted and prohibited areas are in the Washington TCA? Yes, a pilot must try very hard to avoid them, too; a prohibited area (the White House) is directly off the departure end of Runway 36 at Washington National.

Prohibited Area

Airspace clearly depicted on IFR and VFR charts and a pilot is absolutely *not allowed to fly into or through these areas*. This is important to remember because more than a few will hurt you if you trespass.

There are very few prohibited areas but they do exist. Usually they encompass places like Camp David in Maryland or key military locations. Do avoid flying through these areas.

Restricted Areas

These areas prohibit flying only part of the time. Gunnery and bombing ranges, as well as certain military airspace, make up restricted areas. If questions arise about whether or not to fly through one of these areas, ask ATC.

Restricted areas are depicted on aeronautical charts with dimensions, hours of operation, and which controlling facility is in charge.

Walt Garrison

Wander into restricted airspace and you might see government in action!

It seems that the only time these areas are "hot" (active) is when you need to fly through to avoid a line of thunderstorms. They are very often using real bullets and missiles and the military guys aren't looking out for you because they're busy. If you have any doubt about restricted airspace, stay out.

Warning Areas

These are actually restricted areas, but can't be called that by the United States government because they are officially out of U.S. jurisdiction. Warning areas are pieces of airspace that lie outside the legal three-mile limit offshore. Because the airspace is outside the United States and is over international waters it cannot legally be named a restricted area.

It should be considered the same thing because identical activity occurs in a warning area that transpires in a restricted area: supersonic fighters shooting real missiles and guns. Stay away.

Military Operations Areas (MOA)

These blocks of airspace are used by the military primarily for training flights. An IFR flight *can* be cleared through this airspace by ATC as long as ATC can provide separation from the participating military traffic. For example, if the military guys were going to fly below FL 240, ATC could clear a civilian flight at FL 330 without a problem. If unable, ATC is required to route traffic around the MOA.

VFR traffic is required to avoid MOA if it is active. The FAA recommends contacting ATC within 100 nm of MOA to see if it is active.

Military pilots operating in a MOA are usually performing aerobatics: the main reason this airspace was created. Military pilots in a MOA are exempt from FAR Part 91.71, the regulation that prohibits aerobatic flight on federal airways.

Alert Area

These parcels of airspace depicted on charts inform pilots about unusual activity like flight training or parachute jumps. Pilots and participants in the unusual activity should look out for each other.

4

Airport Radar Service Area

THE AIRPORT RADAR SERVICE AREA IS THE MOST LIKELY PLACE in which you will find yourself in the crowded skies of the United States of America.

Although the TCA gets the most attention in discussions about air traffic conditions, it is a fact of life that only nine Group I TCAs and 14 Group II TCAs exist. Presently 126 ARSAs are active in the United States, with more planned.

WHAT IS AN ARSA?

Basically, an ARSA is a formal version of a formerly informal procedure. Before the existence of the TRSA (Terminal Radar Service Area) and the ARSA, it was common for VFR pilots to request radar service from approach controls and en route centers. The controllers would then provide traffic advisories and other services like navigational assistance to the pilots on request, work load permitting.

The trouble with this approach was twofold. First, there was no standard way for the pilot and controller to function; service varied from location to location and a pilot was never quite sure how to go about asking for help. Second, there was no formal requirement for the controller to help; the service was based solely on whether or not the controller's work load permitted.

Another problem was that in areas of high traffic volume, where ARSAs now exist, many of the pilots could traverse these busy areas without contacting approach control or any controlling facility unless they entered an airport traffic control area.

The intent and design of the ARSA solves these problems, recognizing the fact that it is important to provide radar to VFR and IFR pilots in congested areas. The ARSA standardizes operations in the areas and mandates that the controllers must handle all traffic, not a work load permitting basis as in the past.

WHAT ABOUT TRSAs?

A TRSA (Terminal Radar Service Area) is basically an ARSA with no requirement for pilots to participate, or, for that matter, any other rules.

The same services are provided by controllers to pilots who do participate, but the effectiveness of this is diluted by the fact that many other pieces of traffic might be present in a TRSA that the controller might neither see nor have any control over.

TRSA service is divided: Stage II and Stage III.

In Stage II service radar *advisories* are provided on a *work load permitting* basis. Also, participating VFR aircraft are sequenced into and out of the airport traffic pattern.

Stage III service provides radar *separation* of VFR traffic as well as sequencing. In a Stage III situation you must maintain certain minimum altitudes in order to receive the radar service.

Once again it is important to note that in a TRSA not all aircraft are required to participate. There is absolutely no guarantee that you are safe from other traffic.

A TRSA is shown on VFR charts as a set of two magenta circles with an inner area that usually overlaps a control area and a wider outside area.

Airport radar service areas in the United States.

ALABAMA	Phoenix	Castle AFB (Merced)
Birmingham	Tucson	El Toro MCAS
Huntsville		Fresno
Mobile	**ARKANSAS**	March AFB
	Little Rock	Mather AFB
ALASKA		McClellan AFB
Anchorage	**CALIFORNIA**	Monterey
	Beale AFB	Norton AFB
ARIZONA	Burbank	Oakland
Davis-Monthan AFB		

Ontario
Sacramento
Santa Barbara

COLORADO
Colorado Springs

CONNECTICUT
Windsor Locks (Bradley)

DISTRICT OF COLUMBIA
Washington (Dulles)

FLORIDA
Pensacola
Whiting NAS
Pensacola NAS
Daytona Beach
Ft. Lauderdale
Ft. Myers
Jacksonville
Orlando
West Palm Beach
Sarasota
Tallahassee (Municipal)
Tampa

GEORGIA
Columbus
Savannah

HAWAII
Kahului

IDAHO
Boise

ILLINOIS
Champaign
Chicago (Midway)
Moline
Peoria
Springfield

INDIANA
Evansville
Fort Wayne
Indianapolis
South Bend

IOWA
Cedar Rapids
Des Moines

KANSAS
Wichita

KENTUCKY
Covington (Cincinnati, OH)
Lexington
Louisville

LOUISIANA
Barksdale AFB
Baton Rouge
Lafayette
Shreveport

MAINE
Portland

MARYLAND
Baltimore

MICHIGAN
Flint
Grand Rapids
Lansing

MISSISSIPPI
Columbus AFB
Jackson

NEBRASKA
Lincoln
Omaha
Offutt AFB

NEVADA
Reno

NEW JERSEY
Atlantic City (Intl)

NEW MEXICO
Albuquerque

NEW YORK
Albany
Buffalo

Islip
Rochester
Syracuse

NORTH CAROLINA
Charlotte
Fayetteville
Greensboro
Pope AFB (Fayetteville)
Raleigh/Durham

OHIO
Akron
Columbus
Cincinnati (Covington,KY)
Dayton
Toledo

OKLAHOMA
Oklahoma City
Tinker AFB
Tulsa

OREGON
Portland

PENNSYLVANIA
Allentown

PUERTO RICO
San Juan

RHODE ISLAND
Providence

SOUTH CAROLINA
Charleston (AFB/Intl)
Columbia
Greer
Shaw AFB

TENNESSEE
Chattanooga
Knoxville
Memphis
Nashville

TEXAS
Abilene

Fig. 4-1. Continued.

Amarillo
Austin
Corpus Christi
Dallas (Love)
Dyess AFB (Abilene)
El Paso
Houston (William P. Hobby)
Laughlin AFB
Lubbock
Midland
San Antonio

UTAH
Salt Lake City

VERMONT
Burlington

VIRGINIA
Norfolk
Richmond
Roanoke

WASHINGTON
Spokane (Intl)

Spokane (Fairchild AFB)
Whidbey Island (NAS)

WEST VIRGINIA
Charleston

WISCONSIN
Green Bay
Madison
Milwaukee

PILOT'S RESPONSIBILITY

It would probably be a good idea at this point to review the pilot's responsibility when operating in a TRSA or ARSA or any airspace where clearances and advisories are given by ATC. It is listed in boldface in AIM Part One:

> "These programs (TRSAs and ARSAs) are not to be interpreted as relieving pilots of their responsibilities to see and avoid other traffic operating in basic VFR weather conditions, to adjust their operations and flight path as necessary to preclude serious wake encounters to maintain appropriate terrain and obstruction clearance or to remain in weather conditions equal to or better than the minimums required by FAR 91.105. Whenever compliance with an assigned route, heading and/or altitude is likely to compromise pilot responsibility respecting terrain and obstruction clearance, vortex exposure, and weather minimums, approach control should be so advised and a revised clearance or instruction obtained."

Also, keep in mind that even on an IFR clearance the choice of whether or not it should be followed is yours. It is unsafe to follow an IFR clearance given by ATC it is your responsibility as pilot-in-command to do the safe thing; advise ATC and get an alternate clearance.

ARSA DIMENSIONS

There is no mystery about the dimension of ARSAs, which is spelled out very neatly in FAR Parts 71 and 91.

A basic, standard ARSA design is changed only by specific, on site variations.

The airspace of an ARSA is based on two circles, both centered on the ARSA's primary airport. The inner circle of the ARSA has a five nautical mile radius, the same size as the airport traffic control area that it overlaps. The inner circle's upper limit is 4,000 ft. AGL, 1,000 feet above the ceiling of the airport traffic control area.

The outer circle has a radius of 10 nautical miles. Its vertical dimensions begin at 1,200 ft. AGL and tops out even with the ceiling of the inner circle at 4,000 ft.

OUTER AREA

In addition to the ARSA there is an outer area, beginning at the 10 nautical mile limit of the ARSA and extending 20 nautical miles. The outer area's floor is the lower limit of radar and radio coverage for that area; it rises to the ceiling of the respective approach control area.

ARSAs are depicted on VFR charts, such as sectionals, by a slashed blue line. They are also depicted on some terminal control area charts.

Airport Radar Service Area (ARSA)

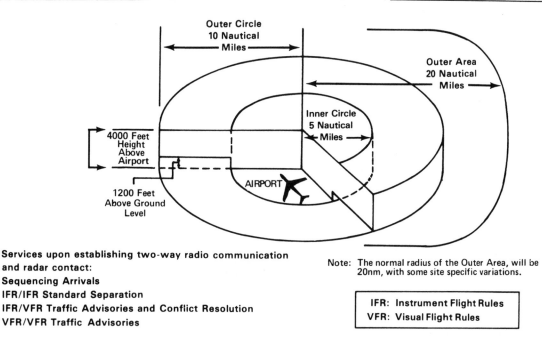

Services upon establishing two-way radio communication
and radar contact:

Sequencing Arrivals

IFR/IFR Standard Separation

IFR/VFR Traffic Advisories and Conflict Resolution

VFR/VFR Traffic Advisories

Note: The normal radius of the Outer Area, will be 20nm, with some site specific variations.

IFR: Instrument Flight Rules
VFR: Visual Flight Rules

FAA's standard ARSA design.

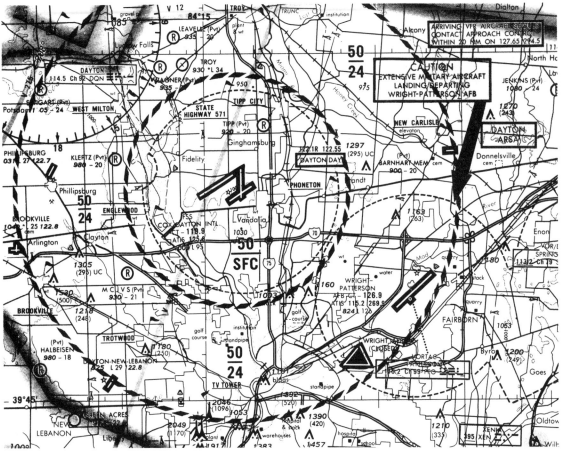

A typical ARSA (Dayton) depicted on a VFR sectional chart.

Where are they on IFR en route charts? Nowhere, because you are already operating with ATC two-way radio communications and operating on an ATC clearance: no need to know exactly when and where you enter an ARSA airspace.

OPERATING IN AN ARSA

Good news regarding rules for operating in and out of an ARSA: it's easy. Let's run down the rules and then go into more detail.

Pilot Certification

There is no specific certification required to operate an aircraft in an ARSA. Pilots from student through airline transport pilot are perfectly welcome in an ARSA.

Remember, there is no requirement for an aircraft to be flown by an instrument rated pilot because an ARSA serves IFR and VFR traffic, especially VFR traffic because even without an ARSA, controllers are required to service IFR traffic.

A student pilot on a solo training flight may operate in an ARSA if the rules discussed later in the chapter are followed. A student will get along fine and will have the added advantage of ATC looking over their shoulder ready to help with vectors back to the airport if they get disoriented.

The professional pilot and the pilot operating on an IFR flight plan get help to avoid VFR traffic. This is especially valuable in marginal or scuzzy VFR conditions.

Equipment Required

The only equipment required for operation in an ARSA is a two-way radio. Neither the AIM nor the FARs specify that a radio must be a VHF or UHF transmitter, but they do very clearly state that while operating in an ARSA the pilot must maintain two-way radio communication with the controlling facility.

ARRIVALS AND OVERFLIGHTS

Let's take a minute to see what FAR 91.88 says about flying into or through an ARSA: No person may operate an aircraft in an airport radar service area unless two-way radio communication is established with ATC prior to entering that area and is thereafter maintained with ATC while within that area.

You may have already noticed that nowhere in the FARs, AIM, or even this book has anybody mentioned anything about a "clearance." All the rules say about flying into or through an ARSA is "two-way communications must be maintained with ATC."

Although ATC controls sequencing in and out of the ARSA's primary airport, they have no power to clear you to do anything that has to do with the ARSA. In other words, if called prior to entering the ARSA, ATC cannot turn you back nor deny clearance through the ARSA; ATC can only deny sequencing into the traffic pattern at the primary airport and issue traffic warnings if you are VFR.

PRIMARY AIRPORT

According to the FAA, the primary airport "is the airport designated in Part 71, Subpart L, for which the airport radar service area is designated. A satellite airport is any other airport within the airport radar service area." The Tallahassee ARSA primary airport is Tallahassee Municipal Airport.

A satellite airport might lie well within the ARSA, however, there is only one primary airfield per ARSA.

When departing a primary airport, no pilot may operate without maintaining two-way communication at all times with ATC. The rule at satellite airports, according to the FAA is: "Aircraft departing satellite airports/heliports within the ARSA surface area shall establish two-way communication with ATC a soon as possible. Pilots must comply with approved FAA traffic patterns when departing these airports."

In other words, if the controlling facility (approach control) is at another airport miles away from the satellite airport, usually it is physically impossible to establish two-way communication with ATC due to line of sight restrictions. Also, it wouldn't be very safe. It is far wiser when flying out of a small airport to monitor unicom than talking with a radar controller 10 miles away who can't see a radar return due to ground clutter.

When arriving at a secondary airport that has a control tower, ATC will hand you off to that tower in plenty of time to establish communications.

ULTRALIGHTS

Ultralights usually are not welcome within the confines of ARSAs. FAR Part 103 has a ruling:

"No person may operate an ultralight vehicle within an airport radar service area unless that person has prior permission from the air traffic control facility having jurisdiction over that airspace."

It would seem, then, that the same controlling facility that issues a clearance in and through the ARSA has the power of exclusion if flying an ultralight, even with a two-way radio.

PARACHUTE JUMPING

According to FAR Part 105:

"No person may make a parachute jump and no pilot-in-command may allow a parachute jump to be made from that aircraft in or into an airport radar service area without, or in violation of, the terms of an ATC authorization."

It looks like if you want to go for a quick parachute jump you must do it in some other place. This makes sense because remember that one of

Ultralights aren't usually welcome visitors in an ARSA.

ATC's functions in an ARSA is the separation of traffic and the avoidance of collisions. It is impossible to control a person hanging from a parachute, and it is unlikely that they would be carrying a two-way radio or would be able to follow a traffic advisory even if ATC could issue one.

ATC SERVICES PROVIDED

Air traffic control has four major responsibilities within the ARSA. The first and probably most important is the sequencing of all arriving and departing aircraft to and from the primary airport.

Because all ARSA primary airports are controlled by a control tower, the requirement of sequencing arriving VFR and IFR aircraft is assumed. It is to ATC advantage, though, that it can establish contact and communicate with VFR aircraft a little farther out (usually 20 nm) and get them in line and advise them of traffic sooner.

The second requirement, maintaining IFR separation of IFR aircraft, is something ATC does everywhere anyway. All the usual requirements of keeping IFR aircraft a certain distance and altitude away from each other applies in an ARSA just like all other controlled airspace.

The third thing required of ATC in an ARSA is probably the most important to IFR and VFR pilots. Controllers are charged with the responsibility of separating IFR and VFR aircraft within an ARSA. ATC issues traffic advisories and vectors to the conflicting aircraft so that radar targets don't touch and at least 500 feet vertical separation is maintained. This gives the pilot a little more protection than in a non-ARSA environment. If you are IFR and are just about to break out of the clouds at 3,000 ft., you can rest a little easier in an ARSA that you probably won't be surprised by a VFR aircraft just below the cloud base.

Keep in mind, though, that 500 feet separation is not much separation at all. Also, two radar targets "not touching" could mean a very close call.

The last requirement for ATC within the ARSA is providing traffic advisories and safety alerts to VFR aircraft. Notice no requirement to maintain any separation between VFR aircraft, . . . only to advise about conflict.

SERVICE IN THE OUTER AREA

Identical services are provided by the controller in the outer area around an ARSA as long as two-way radio communication is established with the aircraft involved. Remember there is no requirement in the outer area to contact anybody and for that reason there might be a lot of traffic that isn't talking with ATC. The controller will try to point out the traffic anyway but won't have information on type or altitude.

If departing an ARSA and flying into the outer area, ATC will assume continued service into this area unless told otherwise. Outside the inner circle you can refuse or discontinue the service any time.

Controller assistance within the outer circle might be shut off by the controller if the work load is too great to provide service to both IFR and VFR traffic.

OPERATING IN AN ARSA

The first question that arises when pilots talk about operating in an ARSA is "Do I really have to comply with ATC when flying through an

ARSA? After all, the FARs only say that *two-way radio communication with ATC will be maintained*, never anything about issuing a clearance."

There is a "catch 22" to this situation. Sure, it only says that a pilot has to maintain two-way communication while in an ARSA and really doesn't say he must get a clearance to operate in one.

What happens when ATC replies:

"Roger 123 Yankee, maintain VFR at 3,500 feet and turn left to heading one three zero?"

In effect, even though you are VFR, the controller has issued a clearance. Do they have that right? It is a gray area in the regulations, but covered by FAR Part 91.75:

(a) When an ATC clearance has been obtained, no pilot in command may deviate from that clearance, except in an emergency, unless he obtains an amended clearance. However, except in positive controlled airspace, this paragraph does not prohibit him from canceling an IFR flight plan if he is operating in VFR weather conditions. If a pilot is uncertain of the meaning of an ATC clearance, he shall immediately request clarification from ATC."

That paragraph implies that you only get a clearance from ATC when operating on an IFR flight plan and in IFR weather. The next paragraph is the kicker and is the gray area I previously referred to:

"(b) Except in an emergency, no person may, in an area in which air traffic control is exercised, operate an aircraft contrary to an ATC instruction."

Well, an ARSA is certainly an area in which air traffic control is exercised. So a basic clearance like an altitude and heading issued while operating VFR in VFR weather must be accepted or be in violation of FARs.

Air traffic control certainly cannot issue a clearance for something that is either against FARs or would create an emergency.

Let's say that a clearance would put you in the clouds. As a VFR pilot this is an emergency, right? Even if you are IFR-rated and flying an aircraft capable of flying through those clouds, it would not be proper nor legal to accept that clearance. Either it would be an emergency or a violation of the regs depending on ratings and experience. Either way, you are not required to follow that clearance.

You *are* required to tell the controller that you are unable to follow the clearance and explain why. ATC will probably find a solution.

TWO-WAY RADIO COMMUNICATION

You are about to enter an ARSA and try to contact the proper controller on the proper frequency, stating position, altitude, and heading. The controller responds: "Aircraft calling, please standby."

Was that radio contact enough to enter the ARSA? According to the FAA, two-way radio communication never took place because the controller never responded to the identification.

If the controller said: "Roger 123 Yankee, please standby," that *does* constitute radio communication, and you can enter the ARSA.

Nowadays the controller is required to file a report when a violation occurs. Whether or not they actually do issue a violation depends on whether there was a traffic conflict, and other factors, like whether or not a supervisor was standing behind the controller when the violation occurred.

TCA, ARSA, TRSA, AND SELECTED RADAR APPROACH CONTROL FREQUENCIES

ATLANTA TCA	EAST OF V97 NORTH OF V18 119.3 OR 381.6 SOUTH OF V18 119.8 OR 343.6 WEST OF V97 NORTH OF V18 121.0 OR 385.5
BIRMINGHAM ARSA	132.2 385.6 (050°-230°) 124.5 338.2 (231°-049°)
CHARLOTTE ARSA	126.15 316.7 (360°-179°) 125.35 257.2 (180°-359°)
CHATTANOOGA ARSA	125.1 379.1 (016°-195°) 119.2 321.2 (196°-015°)
COLUMBIA ARSA	118.2 338.2 (110°-289°) 124.9 285.6 (290°-109°)
COLUMBUS ARSA	126.0 226.4 (001°-150°) 126.55 278.5 (151°-240°) 125.5 388.0 (241°-360°)
GREER ARSA	119.4 350.2 EAST 118.8 385.4 WEST
HUNTSVILLE ARSA	125.6 354.1 (360°-179°) 118.05 239.0 (180°-359°)
KNOXVILLE ARSA	118.0 360.8 (051°-229°) 123.9 353.6 (230°-050°)
NASHVILLE ARSA	124.0 360.7 (019°-199°) 120.6 388.0 (200°-018°)
SAVANNAH ARSA	125.3 387.1 (011°-109°) 118.4 354.0 (110°-269°) 120.4 388.8 (270°-010°)
ASHEVILLE TRSA	124.65 351.8 (160°-339°) 125.8 226.8 (340°-159°)
AUGUSTA TRSA	119.15 231.1 (350°-169°) 126.8 270.3 (170°-349°)
MACON TRSA	119.6 388.2 (130°-329° ABOVE 5000 FT) 124.2 279.6 (330°-129° ABOVE 5000 FT) 124.8 324.3 (ALL SECTORS 5000 FT AND BELOW)
MONTGOMERY TRSA	124.0 319.9 (SOUTH) 125.3 369.2 (NORTH)
LAWSON AAF RADAR	126.55 278.5

TCA, TRSA, and ARSA air traffic control frequencies appear in the margin of a sectional chart.

ESTABLISHING CONTACT

When flying out of the primary airport, contact with the controlling facility is as easy as monitoring ATIS (Automatic Terminal Information Service), calling ground control and getting underway.

The tower controller will hand you to the departure controller and you are more or less automatically in the system.

If you happen to be flying out of a secondary airport in an ARSA, establishing contact with ATC is a little harder but not too difficult. The proper frequency to contact controllers may be obtained from several sources.

The first would be a reliable sectional chart. ARSAs have a frequency box just outside the airspace depicted on the chart directing contact with ATC on a discreet frequency.

A TRSA has a small box outside the depicted airspace telling you to look up the ATIS frequency or the tower frequency in the tab located next to the airport.

Even with the additional protection offered by the radar coverage in ARSAs, it is a good idea to keep eyes open.

On VFR navigational charts, the ARSA is depicted as a scalloped magenta line. TRSAs are shown as a solid magenta line around the airspace. TRSAs and ARSAs are not shown on IFR charts because it is unnecessary. Every requirement of a VFR pilot in an ARSA is absorbed when IFR.

Probably the most important change on the horizon for operating in an ARSA will be the new encoding altimeter rule. The FAA proposes that by December 30, 1990, all aircraft operating in or out of an ARSA will be required to have an encoding altimeter.

Also included in this rule change will be a requirement by July 1, 1989, that all aircraft operating within 30 miles of a TCA or above ten thousand feet must also have an encoding altimeter.

Anyway you cut it, the ARSA seems to be the "wave of the future," and you will find yourself flying in and through them quite a bit in the future.

5
Terminal Control Area

BACK DURING THE "GOOD OLD DAYS" OF AVIATION, YOU COULD FLY an airplane just about anywhere in the country. Even a 65-horse engine, no radio, and rag-wing plane had every legal right to land at places like Chicago's O'Hare or New York's Kennedy just about any time of the day.

Two developments during the 1960s lead to changes: increased traffic load at these places and the advent of the jet airliner.

Both developments in aviation history presented a problem and the flying public (non-pilot voters) demanded safer skies, especially around major terminal areas.

This public demand for more control, plus new technology radars, combined to start the age of the terminal control area.

After June 25, 1970, radio-free, transponder-free airplanes could no longer fly anywhere; the TCA became a fact of life at 21 of the airports in the United States.

Was it onerous over-regulation of our nation's skies? Maybe, but having TCAs around nowadays is simply something we Americans live with, like the IRS and all the taxes on fuel. As a matter of fact, after all these years since their inception, there are only two additional TCAs than in 1970.

Before you get all excited, keep in mind that the airspace that was considered a "TCA Group III" is now usually designated as an ARSA.

Strangely enough, even though ARSAs outnumber TCAs by a factor of at least five, most pilots are really upset about TCAs and hardly ever mention ARSAs.

Ask most pilots about flying into the ARSA at Des Moines and they will answer "No problem!" with a sly grin on their weathered faces. Mention flying into the Group I TCA in Miami and they will dive under the table in fear.

The only real difference between the two types of airspace is that most of us have a lot of experience flying in and out of ARSAs and very little experience operating in and out of TCAs. Let's unwrap this onion of a subject, wipe away our tears, and take away some of the myth and muck this subject usually entails.

WHAT IS A TCA?

According to the FAA:

"A Terminal Control Area (TCA) consists of controlled airspace extending upward from the surface or higher to specified altitudes, within which **all aircraft** are subject to the operating rules and pilot and equipment requirements specified in FAR 91. Terminal control area structure and characteristics are described in FAR 71. Each TCA location is designated as either a Group I or Group II TCA, and includes at least one primary airport around which the TCA is located."

As usual, the FAA crammed 10 minutes of information into a five-day seminar. Simply stated, if you are in a TCA, no matter what you are flying, from a lawn chair attached to weather balloons to a Boeing 747 SP, you are required to follow certain rules, and two types of TCA exist.

LOCATIONS

Nine are Group I TCAs:

Atlanta	Boston	Los Angeles
Chicago	Dallas	San Francisco
Miami	New York	Washington, D.C.

Fourteen are Group II TCAs:

Cleveland	Kansas City	Pittsburgh
Denver	Las Vegas	Seattle
Detroit	Minneapolis	St. Louis
Honolulu	New Orleans	San Diego
Houston	Philadelphia	

It is pretty clear how the FAA determines which areas are designated "Group I" and which areas are "Group II." The top nine represent the busiest, most crowded airspace in the United States, if you don't count Oshkosh, Wisconsin, or Lakeland, Florida, during the yearly EAA fly-ins.

The logic of the FAA is that crowded and complex airspace demands complex rules for aircraft and pilots in that airspace.

Unlike ARSAs, which are only depicted on VFR charts, TCAs are shown on sectional, world aeronautical, en route low altitude, DOD FLIP (approach plates), and TCA charts.

A TCA is shown on VFR charts as a series of solid blue lines formed in the shape of the airspace.

Notice two things. First a TCA is much larger than an ARSA. ARSAs can be different sizes, however, they are rarely larger than 20 miles in diameter. The Atlanta TCA is roughly 71 nautical miles in diameter!

Second, quite a few rings in this depiction of the TCA show not only the dimensions of that part of the TCA but also altitudes where the TCA begins and ends. Outer rings show:

$$\frac{125}{100}$$

This simply means that the Atlanta TCA's floor is 10,000 ft. MSL and its ceiling 12,500 ft. MSL.

Don't make the mistake of using the figure on the south side of the TCA, near the range marks. That large 1 with the smaller 6 near it, written in blue might be confusing, but remember that it is a maximum elevation figure (MEF): the highest feature in the area of the chart bounded by ticked lines of latitude and longitude represented in thousands and hundreds of feet above mean sea level. The MEF is based on information available concerning the highest known feature in each quadrangle, including terrain and obstructions (trees, towers, antennas, etc.).

On Jeppesen IFR en route charts, TCAs are depicted by a light blue border that is interspersed with white dots. National Ocean Service charts indicate a TCA with a solid blue screen.

On the low altitude en route chart, just the outside edge of the TCA is shown. None of the altitudes are depicted. High altitude en route charts, "jet route" charts, do not show TCAs because a high altitude represents airspace above Flight Level 180, which is above any TCA airspace.

Department of Defense FLIP charts and certain Jeppesen maps place the TCA on a separate TCA chart. A TCA does not appear on a specific approach plate.

The Boston TCA chart from Jeppesen is a simpler presentation compared to a VFR chart. The Jepp chart shows range circles, major airways, navigational fixes, and floor and ceiling figures are shown on the left-hand side of the chart near the circle borders.

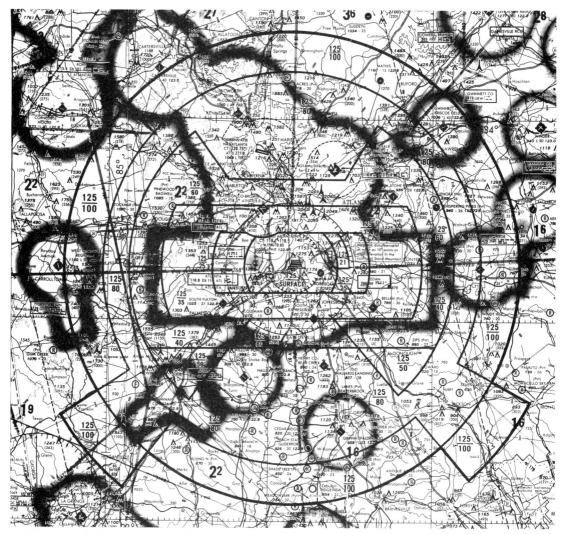

A TCA is much larger than an ARSA.

Notice also on the Boston chart that dimensions as well as the floor and ceiling figures are quite different than Atlanta. In Atlanta, the floor in the outside circle of the TCA is 10,000 ft., Boston is 4,000 ft. Ceilings are also different: Boston 7,000 ft., Atlanta 12,500 ft. This brings up a

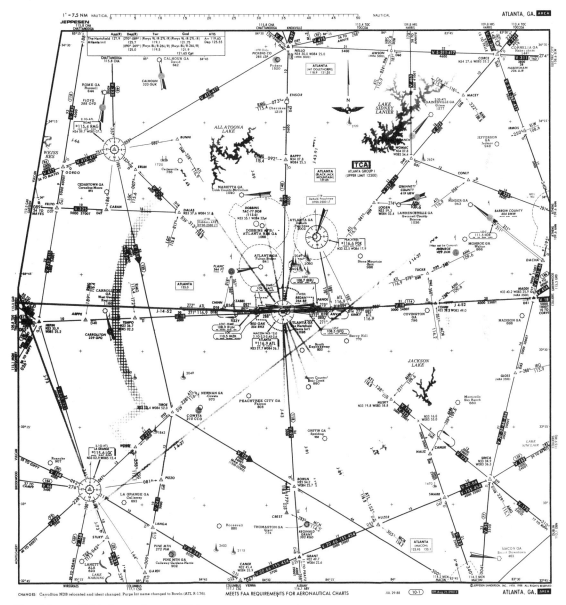

The Atlanta TCA shown in an IFR format. Reproduced with permission of Jeppesen Sanderson, Inc.

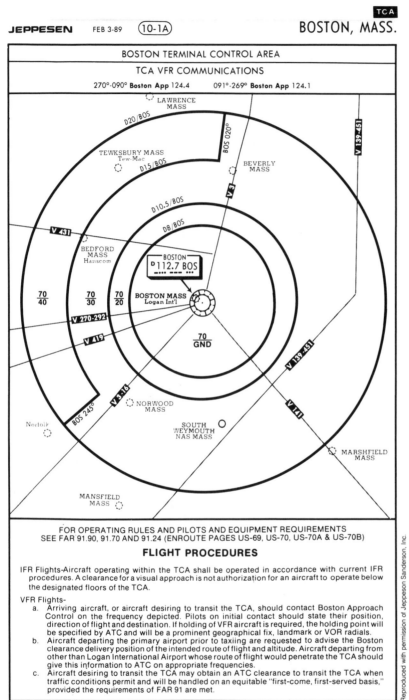

The Boston Terminal Control Area showing frequencies, boundaries, and altitudes.

Within image:

BOSTON TERMINAL CONTROL AREA

TCA VFR COMMUNICATIONS

270°-090° **Boston App** 124.4   091°-269° **Boston App** 124.1

LAWRENCE MASS

D20/BOS

BOS 020°

V 139-451

TEWKSBURY MASS
Tew-Mac

D15/BOS

BEVERLY MASS

V 3

D10.5/BOS

V 431

D8/BOS

BEDFORD MASS
Hanscom

BOSTON
D 112.7 BOS

BOSTON MASS
Logan Int'l

| 70/40 | 70/30 | 70/20 |

V 270-292

V 419

70/GND

V 139-451

V 338

BOS 245°

NORWOOD MASS

Norfolk

SOUTH WEYMOUTH NAS MASS

V 141

MARSHFIELD MASS

MANSFIELD MASS

FOR OPERATING RULES AND PILOTS AND EQUIPMENT REQUIREMENTS
SEE FAR 91.90, 91.70 AND 91.24 (ENROUTE PAGES US-69, US-70, US-70A & US-70B)

FLIGHT PROCEDURES

IFR Flights-Aircraft operating within the TCA shall be operated in accordance with current IFR procedures. A clearance for a visual approach is not authorization for an aircraft to operate below the designated floors of the TCA.

VFR Flights-
  a. Arriving aircraft, or aircraft desiring to transit the TCA, should contact Boston Approach Control on the frequency depicted. Pilots on initial contact should state their position, direction of flight and destination. If holding of VFR aircraft is required, the holding point will be specified by ATC and will be a prominent geographical fix, landmark or VOR radials.
  b. Aircraft departing the primary airport prior to taxiing are requested to advise the Boston clearance delivery position of the intended route of flight and altitude. Aircraft departing from other than Logan International Airport whose route of flight would penetrate the TCA should give this information to ATC on appropriate frequencies.
  c. Aircraft desiring to transit the TCA may obtain an ATC clearance to transit the TCA when traffic conditions permit and will be handled on an equitable "first-come, first-served basis," provided the requirements of FAR 91 are met.

CHANGES: Communications.

very important point about TCAs. All TCAs are generally similar, but specifically distinct. When operating in or around a TCA, be very careful to read the small print.

Equipment Requirements and Operating Rules

The first and main rule for operating in any TCA is "Regardless of weather conditions, ATC authorization is required prior to operating within a TCA."

Unlike other airspace where pilot decisions about obtaining clearances and instructions from air traffic control were predicated on whether weather conditions were VFR or IFR, a pilot is *always operating on an ATC clearance* when flying in a TCA.

Beyond that, equipment requirements and operating rules abound and deserve a review.

EQUIPMENT

No matter what you are flying, an aircraft needs:

- A two-way radio capable of communicating with ATC on appropriate frequencies. This, for civilian pilots, would usually mean a VHF transceiver. "Appropriate frequencies" in most TCAs would mean you would need more than a 90-channel "cheapie" model. ATCs in places like Atlanta operates on unusual frequencies like 127.05 mHz and 121.65 mHz. Those are "appropriate" frequencies and an airplane must be properly equipped.
- A VOR or TACAN receiver. No other navigational equipment is required. Many clearances from ATC while operating in a TCA rely on a VOR navigation signal.
- A 4096-code transponder with Mode C automatic altitude reporting equipment, except for helicopters operating at or below 1,000 ft. AGL under a letter of agreement.

What if you are operating perfectly legal with a transponder and an encoding altimeter when halfway through the TCA the encoder conks out? Or outside the TCA, about to enter, the encoder bites the dust? ATC is allowed, when notified, to authorize a deviation from the altitude reporting equipment requirement.

If the transponder quits before entering the TCA, no. ATC must have at least an hour notice for authorization.

Under both scenarios the key word is *may*. ATC does not *have* to allow that operation. It is up to them, based on their work load, what kind of mood they are in, and how nicely you ask.

PILOT REQUIREMENTS

You must have a private pilot certificate or higher to land or take off from an airport within a TCA.

This brings up two interesting points. A student pilot operating at South Fulton Airport, southwest of Atlanta Hartsfield, is flying within the lateral boundaries of the TCA. But the aircraft must remain below 3,500 ft. MSL to avoid TCA airspace.

A student pilot on a VFR cross-country can fly from South Fulton Airport across the TCA to Stone Mountain Britt Memorial Airport on the northeast side of town as long as he does not land or take off in the TCA, the airplane is properly equipped, and he follows ATC clearances. The rule wasn't made to hassle student pilots, just keep them out of the traffic pattern at Hartsfield.

Miscellaneous Rules

A large turbine-powered airplane flying to or from the primary airport of a TCA is supposed to remain above the TCA floor while within the lateral limits of the TCA.

A "large" turbine-powered airplane would be, by definition, any airplane weighing more than 12,500 pounds.

This rule was made up primarily to protect the good old airliners. If the purpose of the whole TCA is to provide large, airline-type aircraft with added protection and separation from other aircraft, it stands to reason that it would be a good idea to make sure that they stay in that airspace.

Aircraft may not fly in the airspace underneath the TCA at an indicated airspeed of more than 200 knots (230 mph). The speed limit within the TCA is 250 knots: quite different from the maximum speed limit in an airport traffic area of 200 knots, or 1.3 times clean stall speed. The traffic mix in a Group I or Group II TCA is mostly turbine aircraft that regularly operate at 250 knots or more. Because all traffic is capable of going fast and the airspace is crowded, allow them to go and come at a faster rate than you would at a smaller airport with a mix of jets, Cessna 150s, and Aztecs.

Regulation does not prescribe a minimum speed, but don't be surprised if the controller says "Maintain 170 knots until the marker." Operating at 80 knots on final at a busy place like O'Hare creates a problem when followed by seven or eight jets with a minimum approach speed of 140 knots or higher.

GROUP II TCA RULES

A Group II TCA requires the same equipment as in a Group I with one very important and expensive exception—an encoding altimeter is not required. ATC can exempt the transponder requirement if requested an hour ahead of time: no in-the-air exceptions.

The only other difference between a Group I and a Group II TCA is that in a Group II there is no minimum pilot certification required. A student pilot can operate in or out of any airport in the TCA's airspace.

IFR OPERATIONS

If you fly on an IFR flight plan into a TCA there is really nothing to worry about and no extra planning is required. About the only thing the FAA requires you to remember is that if you are flying a large, turbine aircraft that is cleared for a visual approach into the TCA's primary airport, you are *not* cleared to descend below the floor of the TCA.

Special techniques for flying IFR in crowded airspace, like a Group I TCA, are covered in Chapter 8 "Survival Techniques for IFR Pilots."

VFR OPERATIONS

Obviously it is much harder to operate VFR in a TCA than it is to fly in the same airspace on an IFR clearance.

When flying VFR into a TCA, the first chore is to figure out exactly where the TCA begins. Approaching the Atlanta Group I TCA from the southeast, from Milledgeville, Georgia, at an altitude of 6,500 ft. MSL, the exact boundary of the TCA is especially difficult to determine without a DME (distance measuring equipment) on board; assuming you knew the mileage figures, notice that they are not shown on the sectional chart. Mileage figures are indicated on a VFR terminal chart.

According to the FAA: "Arriving flights must contact ATC on the appropriate frequency and in relation to geographical fixes shown on local charts. Although a pilot may be operating beneath the floor of the TCA on initial contact, communications with ATC should be established in relation to the points indicated for spacing and sequencing purposes."

Many times, especially when flying into the primary airport of the TCA, "sequencing" means holding somewhere until ATC can find a spot in the inbound flow. It is a fact of life for the VFR pilot flying a slow aircraft that it is difficult for the controller to make room in a traffic pattern that is flying at more than 170 kts.

Because you are VFR, ATC can't issue a holding fix like IFR traffic. In other words, telling a VFR pilot to hold northeast of an intersection, left turns, 20 mile legs, won't work. ATC will usually issue an easy-to-see visual fix like a shopping center or factory to hold over VFR, until they can work you in.

When the controller issues headings and altitudes for sequencing either into or out of a TCA, he is doing so assuming that a pilot will sing out if he clears you into an illegal situation. In other words, it's the pilot's fault if he lets ATC vector him into a cloud when flying VFR.

The problem with this, as you have probably already figured out, is that it is nearly impossible to get a word in edgewise on the approach frequency. If congestion prevents telling the controller about the cloud, what can be done?

You have no real choice: assume that good old pilot-in-command authority the government has bestowed upon you and do whatever is nec-

You are always operating on an ATC clearance when in a TCA.

essary to avoid the "emergency" of entering that cloud. Believe me, when the controller sees you veer 20 degrees off the heading, you *will* get a call on the radio from that controller. That's when you tell about the cloud.

If you are leaving or transiting the TCA VFR, the FAA encourages you to stay out of the airspace. They want you to operate above or below the TCA's airspace or use one of the VFR corridors set up for that purpose.

That sounds restrictive, but remember if you do decide to get a clearance from ATC and fly your aircraft VFR directly through the TCA you might be able to do that—but with all the vectors necessary to get through the TCA without hitting anybody, it may take four hours.

Another reminder the FAA hands out about operating around a TCA is especially important. We'll quote it verbatim from the *Airman's Information Manual*:

> "Unless otherwise authorized by ATC, each person operating a large turbine-engine-powered airplane to or from a primary airport shall operate at or above the designated floors while within the lateral limits of the TCA."

Walt Garrison

There is no minimum airspeed in a TCA, the maximum is 250 knots.

Which means that if you are flying a large jet-fuel-burning aircraft into a primary airport of a TCA, like O'Hare in Chicago, you can't outsmart the system and avoid it by sneaking under and then popping up for landing.

ULTRALIGHTS

It almost goes without saying, but ultralights are not welcome in TCAs. Like all airport radar service areas you are required to get previous permission form ATC before operating your ultralight in TCA airspace. Don't hold your breath waiting.

SECONDARY AIRPORTS

Many times you will have no interest in flying to the primary airport of a TCA. As a matter of fact, if you're smart you will probably avoid a primary airport in a large TCA unless it is impossible to do so. It is much easier in a general aviation aircraft to get into Peachtree-Dekalb Airport in the Atlanta TCA than it is to fly into Hartsfield. Peachtree-Dekalb caters to general aviation and speed will be compatible with the other traffic, not to mention the fact that wake turbulence will be reduced.

Unless you avoid the TCA airspace completely, which isn't impossible but is difficult, you will have to deal with ATC to enter, even if VFR only.

It's no biggie: expect vectors around the traffic pattern of the primary airport to reach the destination. Sometimes the vectors seem to go away from the destination. It will make more sense to realize that many times the primary airport has traffic strung-out up to 20 miles on final approach.

Even if landing at a secondary airport, flying through TCA airspace requires at least the equipment required for operating in that TCA and an ATC clearance.

Terminal control areas are a fact of life in the United States and will continue for the foreseeable future. Dealing with them is no problem as long as you know the rules and follow them.

Now let's look at the largest, most complex airports in the United States and review some tips on how to operate in and near them.

6
Large Airport Operations

IT IS INTERESTING THAT MANY OF THE LARGE AIRPORTS LIKE CHICAGO'S O'Hare, and Miami International, which are feared the most by general aviation pilots are actually among the easiest in the country to operate into and out of. Several reasons come to mind.

The first is that these airports are set up to handle large volumes of air traffic. It is *normal* for the tower and ground controllers at O'Hare to have 20 or 30 pieces of traffic in mind at the same time. If the same thing happened at Tallahassee Municipal, problems would develop because they aren't trained or equipped to handle such a load. At large airports, being busy and overloaded is the norm, not the exception.

Another reason that flying at a large airport might be easier than you think is the facilities. Almost without exception, these airports are very large, have numerous runways available, and are equipped with the latest in approaches, lighting, and markings.

Probably the biggest exception to the above is Washington's National Airport, considered by airline pilots nationwide as one of the most unsafe, scariest airports to operate a large aircraft in. I'll review the reasons later during a review of all Group I TCA primary airports.

WHY FLY THERE?

This first question is not posed to test courage or ability, or to make fun of light airplane drivers. It really is an important question for anyone considering operating at these large airports. Do you have a good reason for being there? If, for example, you are planning a business trip to Atlanta in the company's Baron it would be a much smarter decision to either fly into Peachtree-Dekalb or Fulton County Airport. Both are set up for general aviation aircraft, have great FBOs (fixed base operators), and cater to business people. They are both closer to the business centers of the city and very rarely have huge lines of aircraft waiting for takeoff.

If you do have a reason for going to these airports, such as dropping off a passenger for a major airline, that is fine; or just flying there once or twice to prove you can is a good reason. Flying into these huge operations all the time to make a political point about "equal access" is a waste of everyone's time.

Sometimes the best way to handle a large airport operation is to chose not to go there at all. With the "preachy" part of this chapter out of the way, let's assume you have a need to use these monster airfields and examine survivability.

EXPERIENCE AND PREPARATION

There are two very important points to keep in mind when operating at a large airport. The first is *experience*. The second is *preparation*.

If you have been operating at an airport for a long time, experience is sometimes all that is necessary to handle complex situations when they arise.

If you are taxiing out at O'Hare on a foggy morning and the ground controller says: "Five-one alpha, runway two-seven right, cargo, inner, wedge, outer circular, jog, two-seven parallel, hold short at wolf road," experience would probably be enough to reach proper point on the airport.

People used to operations at that airport realize the "cutsie" names for the taxiways are the easiest thing in the world; the pilot who doesn't fly there much, believes they are a nightmare.

The second necessity for large airports is preparation. Especially if you lack experience, there is nothing like having all ducks in a row before venturing forth into this complicated world.

Experience negates much of the preparation but without experience there is no substitute for lots and lots and lots of preparation.

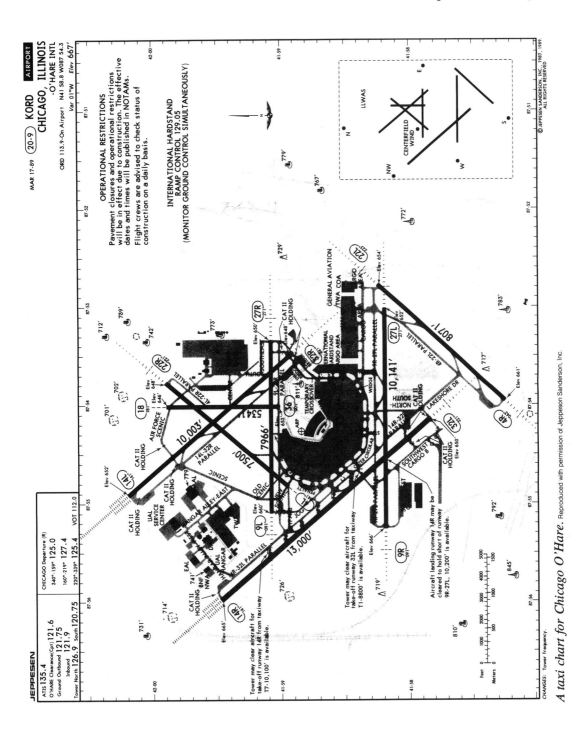

A taxi chart for Chicago O'Hare. Reproduced with permission of Jeppesen Sanderson, Inc.

For the earlier example of a normal taxi-out at O'Hare, instead of experience and a clear mental picture of where the taxiways are, substitute Jeppesen Airways Chart 20-9 and 20-9B for the airport.

It provides all the necessary information, but just having the information isn't enough for an airport like this. If you wait until taxi clearance to discover where you are going, you are already about six years behind the rest of the airport; pull out of the general aviation ramp at Chicago and block the cargo taxiway while searching for the jog and no doubt a Northwest 747 will be sitting right behind you leading a line of five or six jets asking, on the ground control frequency, what you are doing and speculating about your family background.

Preparing for a busy airport doesn't take much study. In the Chicago example, you would have a pretty good idea what runway they were going to assign by listening to the ATIS (automatic terminal information service). Just before you call for taxi clearance look over the taxi chart and get a general idea of where you would be going. It wouldn't hurt to trace the route that ground control recites with a pencil on the chart as they give it.

Prepared means having the charts. There is really no excuse for trying to operate at a large airport without the proper charts. How could you handle the taxi clearance at O'Hare without a taxi chart of some kind, either Jeppesen or NOS? It wouldn't be easy would it? You'd be relegated to asking the controller in a plaintive voice to "Give me a progressive" to the runway.

Not only is this embarrassing, but it is a huge waste of a busy controller's time and might be in violation of the FARs. Remember that mean, old reg (FAR Part 91.5) that says that a pilot has to familiarize himself with all the information pertinent to the flight. It's a "large" regulation that really means that no matter what you do as pilot-in-command anything that goes wrong is basically your fault. Many people point to this regulation as proof that "they're out to get us pilots."

I won't argue this point, but why make it easy for them to nail you? Always have the information necessary to operate at any airport. If you don't have the maps and charts, buy them. If you can't buy them, borrow them, but have them on board before trying to move around a huge airport.

At small, VFR airports, located out in the country, deciding which runway to use is a fairly simple process. You either look at the wind tee or the wind sock to decide the wind direction and then pick the runway that is closest to facing into the wind.

Finding the runway at a small airport can be difficult.

Large airports use basically the same system.

Usually, the runway or runways that are in line with the wind are designated "active." At many airports, though, quite a few other things are taken into consideration when assigning the active runway.

NOISE ABATEMENT

Noise abatement is a major consideration for all airports, but especially those in heavily populated areas.

Boston's Logan International Airport rules state that if the runways are clear and dry, the wind is less than 15 knots, there is a five knot or less *tail wind*, and the weather is VFR, ATC will always assign aircraft takeoffs on Runway 15R and landings on Runway 33L between midnight and 6 a.m. for noise abatement purposes.

71

Suppose you are leaving Boston at 1 a.m. and would like to takeoff into the wind and avoid a three-knot quartering tail wind, can you demand another runway?

Of course. The final authority for runway selection in all cases nationwide always rests with the pilot-in-command. It happens all the time and the controllers don't mind a request for another runway. They *are* required to assign the noise abatement runway, it is then up to the pilot to request a change.

Many times, at places like Boston, airliners have to request another runway for reasons of weight or weather. A Boeing 727 that is going to Dallas, Texas, with a full load of passengers and the fuel required for a bad weather day might be too heavy to take off from the noise abatement runway and the pilot would request a longer runway that was more into the wind. A general aviation pilot in a Cessna 310 might feel very uncomfortable taking off with a five-knot tail wind and would ask for another runway. Either way, the controller should issue another choice assuming there is one.

Don't be surprised if you must accept a long delay in exchange for the new runway. If 20 planes are lined up for the active and you are the only

Waiting out a runway change delay with both engines shut down.

one waiting for the other runway, you will still have to wait for a turn and might have to wait even longer due to other traffic considerations.

Another factor in runway selection for large airports is traffic flow. It is a well-known old saying in Chicago that the controllers launch traffic in the flight's direction and land traffic in the direction they arrive, no matter what the weather is. ATC would deny it, but if you fly there for a while, you do tend to notice that kind of pattern.

FREQUENCY CONGESTION

When trying to call ATC at a large, busy airport it seems nearly impossible to be heard over the dozens of other pilots trying to do the same thing. When you do manage to get ATC's attention, they issue a 10-minute-long clearance and before there is a chance to read any of it back (assuming you got it in the first place) they are talking to somebody else.

Be polite and wait until there is a lull in the action to make your message heard. This is nice and I'm sure Miss Manners would approve of this approach. The trouble is that in some locations, you would grow old and gray before making that first radio call; at busy airports there simply is no "dead air" on the local frequencies.

A second and often-used technique is interrupt and step on somebody. It's never pretty, but many times it is unavoidable and necessary. Usually you won't even be aware of it because three other people are trying to talk on the frequency at the very same time. If lucky, your radio prevails and the controller hears the call.

Obviously, I'm not recommending that jumping all over somebody else's radio call, I'm just saying that when a break occurs, even if it's only for a split second, take it!

One trick I've learned that might help is probably dirty, but it works for me. I've learned over the years that when the frequency is busy with dozens of pilots talking over each other the longest transmission is answered. If two pilots are asking for taxi clearance, the pilot that stays on the air the longest is the last one the controller heard and will probably be the first one he answers.

If a pilot merely says "One-five alpha, taxi" and another says "Miami ground, Cessna three-two bravo taxi from the general aviation ramp please," the controller will more than likely reply: "Aircraft calling for taxi from the general aviation ramp, say again." Because the first part of both transmissions was lost in a loud squeal, ATC heard the longer transmission. It's a rotten trick to play, especially when everything is busy, but it seems to work.

Does talking faster help when you are operating in and out of busy airports? A one word answer for that is *no*.

When flying around these places, notice that the better controllers seem to handle tons of traffic without rushing or a pressing concern. They speak in quiet, calm, and steady words. They usually only have to say things once because they are easy to understand. Contrast this with the controller or pilot who transmits so quickly on the radio in a hurried and worried manner.

You'll probably notice that these people frequently have to repeat themselves, sometimes more than once. They are in such a hurry to get all the information out that they waste about half of their time repeating themselves to the confused pilots that couldn't understand them.

The better, more professional pilots sound calm and deliberate on the radio when all hell is breaking loose around them. I don't mean a false Yeager-drawl, a fake calm; it sounds good in the movies and might sell spark plugs and batteries but is unnecessary for a professional pilot.

Make yourself understood the first time around by using concise, well-thought-out phrasing and you are way ahead of most other pilots in the world, and will gain the respect of every controller.

When the ground controller at O'Hare issues a rapid-fire taxi clearance some pilots read it back and some don't. It is up to the pilot. At many airports the ATIS specifies that for the clearance frequency a pilot should only read back the full clearance if there is a question about it or if company policy dictates it. Many clearance readbacks at most large airports are a simple recitation of the transponder squawk. You might notice airline pilots doing this at smaller airports, when it isn't really necessary, out pure habit.

The main thing about clearances, whether initial IFR clearance at LAX or taxi instructions at Topeka is to *understand* and *follow* them, not that you read them back correctly.

A proper readback of the O'Hare taxi clearance might be a simple "Five-one alpha, roger. If partially misunderstood, say: "Five-one alpha got every part except what you want me to hold short of." Simple. It works.

The fact that the controller sees a pilot doing what he or she was cleared to do is more than enough backup if they are busy. It might do more harm than good to clog up the frequency with a readback of everything.

About the only radio call or clearance they definitely *do* want read back is any hold-short instruction. They usually explain this on the ATIS, but it is always a good idea to read hold-short instructions. Crossing active runways and taxiways is a leading cause of near-misses and actual collisions on the airport. It is very important to know when you are cleared to cross something.

If you don't understand what was said, save a lot of heartache and letter writing and take a minute to ask for a repeat or clarification.

TEMPERS

One last point before reviewing the nine busiest airports in the United States. Do you think people are out to get you? If you don't wonder now, you are guaranteed to get that feeling at into many of these airports.

During the years I've been flying into these places I sometimes think I've heard everything and seen everything possible. I'm usually proven wrong in just a few minutes. I've seen airline pilots cut off other airline pilots at taxiways by speeding up and swerving just to get in front; I've heard people cussing out other people on the radio because they thought they didn't get a fair shake in one way or another.

This will not become a book of proper pilot manners. The point I want to make is that none of the stuff these people have done has changed anything in the least. No matter how much they complain to the controller, they still get off the ground about the same time they were supposed to. No matter how many people cut in line, eventually they will either run off a taxiway into the mud or have a heart attack because they're so uptight about being first.

Getting mad while at a large airport when things don't go your way does no good. If anything, it slows everything down because either you are using up precious air time to express personal views, or the controller has to waste time dealing with you.

If you fly into these airports on a regular basis for any time at all, you *will* run into days that your mother warned about. Just kick-back, take a deep breath and remember that in 10 years none of what you are going through will matter at all.

Let's review the nine busiest airports, which are the primary airports at the nation's Group I TCAs.

ATLANTA HARTSFIELD INTERNATIONAL AIRPORT: Approximately 775,000 Annual Operations

An interesting fact about the Atlanta, Georgia, area is that it has no natural boundaries to limit expansion. Other cities like Boston, New

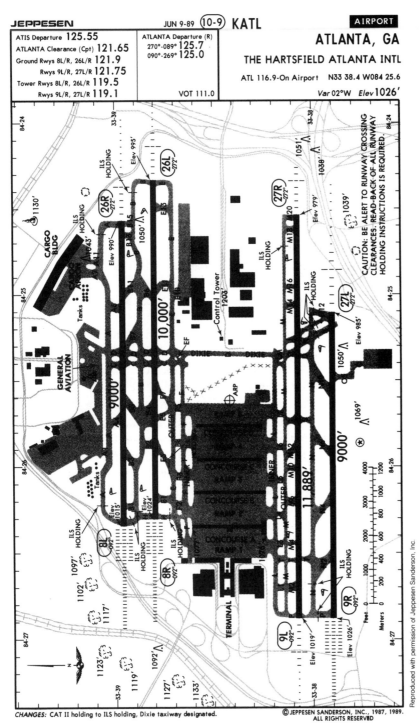

Taxi chart for Hartsfield Atlanta International Airport.

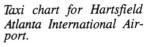

York, Seattle, Chicago, and Los Angeles have a large body of water to curb growth. Denver has mountains to block its expansion. It's conceivable that Atlanta could eventually spread out in all directions.

This isn't true of the airport, Hartsfield International, which is named after an aviation-minded past mayor. The runways and taxiways of Atlanta Hartsfield have just about reached their maximum size. A few years ago the configuration of the runways changed and Runway 9L/27R was extended to a length of almost 12,000 feet, enough for long-range airliners from all over the world to take off and land.

Hartsfield is basically a four-runway airport with every runway running east and west. The airline terminal area is located in the center of the field and tends to dominate all the traffic flow on the airport, both general aviation and air carrier. The general aviation area is on the north side of the airport in what used to be the old airline terminal. Obviously, it is easier for the airliners to get where they are going on the airport.

The inner runways are almost always used for departures and the outside runways are used for landings. Aircraft landing on outer runways initiate a taxi and are usually instructed to hold-short of the inner runways until there is a group of aircraft. They are then cleared to cross while aircraft are held in position prior to takeoff.

Since there are no major bodies of water or mountain ranges around, departures and arrivals occur in all four directions.

The two departures from Atlanta are straightforward. Both involve getting vectored from departure control to a VOR.

ATC expects acceleration to either 250 knots or cruise speed as soon as possible so they can expedite other traffic. Once again, large airports are set up to handle jets and run airport operations accordingly.

IFR arrivals to Atlanta are assigned one of four STARS (standard terminal arrival routes) that correspond to north, south, east, and west. No big surprises here, either, except between the hours of midnight and 6 a.m. it is very rare to get any kind of shortened routing into this airport.

BOSTON'S LOGAN INTERNATIONAL AIRPORT:
Approximately 420,000 Annual Operations

Boston's airport is surrounded on three sides by water and on one side by city. Expect every arrival over water. The most commonly used arrival, the Scupp One, puts you 37 miles east over the Atlantic Ocean, which is something to keep in mind if flying a single-engine airplane to this airport, especially in the winter time.

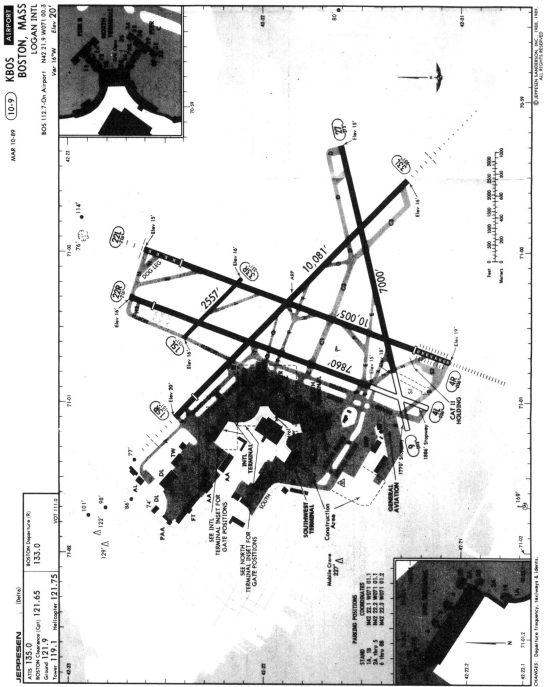

Boston's Logan International. Reproduced with permission of Jeppesen Sanderson, Inc.

CHANGES: Departure frequency, taxiways & idents.

78

Because Boston is just west of the airport, departures in that direction, off Runway 27 require a left turn at the edge of the airport.

There is usually a line for the active runway. General aviation is encouraged to use either the shorter runway, or an intersection, to take off quicker. Once again, it is important and required that a pilot read back all runway and taxiway holding instructions.

Expect the controllers in Boston to be brisk and businesslike. They, like most busy controllers, have little patience with unprofessional pilots, but they are eager to help someone who needs help.

CHICAGO O'HARE INTERNATIONAL AIRPORT: Approximately 795,000 Annual Operations

You've probably guessed by now that this is one of my favorite airports. Located to the west of Chicago, O'Hare was named after a local World War II hero Butch O'Hare. The VOR identifier, ORD, has mystified pilots for as long as I can remember. The story that makes the most sense to me is that the airport is located on what used to be a small village that was named Orchard Grove, thus the ORD identifier.

In spite of, and maybe perhaps because, this place is the busiest airport on the planet, you will find that ATC is not bogged down in procedures at this airport. They tend to do what works. Most large-airport controllers assign slower and slower airspeeds during approach to the field and keep aircraft on a predetermined arrival route. At O'Hare it isn't unusual to have ATC say: "Fly the 32L localizer inbound and *keep your speed up as long as you can*." Because the airport is used almost exclusively by jets capable of 250 knots, the controllers at Chicago have figured out that they can handle more aircraft if flown faster.

Most of the time, departing O'Hare follows the same pattern. ATC usually wants you to speed up as soon as you can to get the heck out of their airspace. When handed over to Indianapolis Center, *they slow you down* for "sequencing" almost every time.

O'Hare arrivals utilize navigational fixes on the four points of the compass. Keep in mind, if flying a single-engine airplane, that at least one of these commonly used routes extends quite a few miles over Lake Michigan; ditching in the winter could be hazardous.

This airport, like all the others, has preferred runways for noise abatement. If landing at O'Hare between ll p.m. and 7 a.m. expect to use Runway 14R; if departing during those hours, you will be assigned Runway 27L.

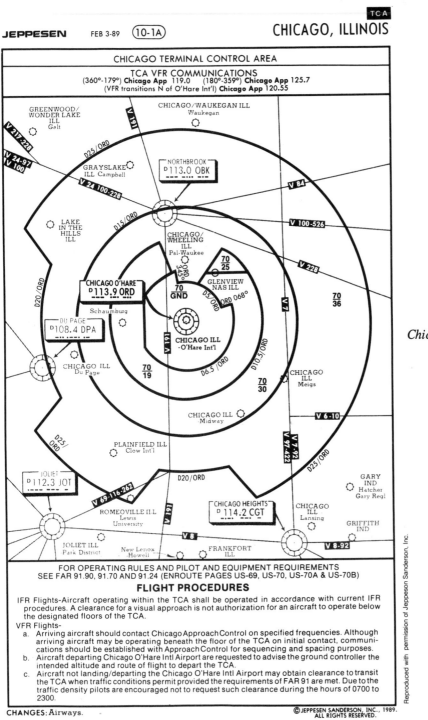

Chicago's TCA.

JEPPESEN FEB 3-89 (10-1A) TCA CHICAGO, ILLINOIS

CHICAGO TERMINAL CONTROL AREA

TCA VFR COMMUNICATIONS
(360°-179°) **Chicago App** 119.0   (180°-359°) **Chicago App** 125.7
(VFR transitions N of O'Hare Int'l) **Chicago App** 120.55

FOR OPERATING RULES AND PILOT AND EQUIPMENT REQUIREMENTS
SEE FAR 91.90, 91.70 AND 91.24 (ENROUTE PAGES US-69, US-70, US-70A & US-70B)

FLIGHT PROCEDURES

IFR Flights-Aircraft operating within the TCA shall be operated in accordance with current IFR
procedures. A clearance for a visual approach is not authorization for an aircraft to operate below
the designated floors of the TCA.

VFR Flights-

a. Arriving aircraft should contact Chicago Approach Control on specified frequencies. Although
   arriving aircraft may be operating beneath the floor of the TCA on initial contact, communications should be established with Approach Control for sequencing and spacing purposes.

b. Aircraft departing Chicago O'Hare Intl Airport are requested to advise the ground controller the
   intended altitude and route of flight to depart the TCA.

c. Aircraft not landing/departing the Chicago O'Hare Intl Airport may obtain clearance to transit
   the TCA when traffic conditions permit provided the requirements of FAR 91 are met. Due to the
   traffic density pilots are encouraged not to request such clearance during the hours of 0700 to
   2300.

CHANGES: Airways.

When departing any time of day expect a right turn after takeoff. Sometimes these turns are more than 90° of heading change and the controllers want it *right now*. Of course, don't make the turn until it is safe, but do make that turn as soon as possible. It is a good idea to brief passengers about the turn because it can be dramatic and more than one passenger has thought they were about to crash when the wing dipped.

DALLAS-FT. WORTH INTERNATIONAL AIRPORT:
Approximately 576,000 Annual Operations

DFW is a *huge* airport. It has seven runways, countless taxiways and two major airlines that dominate the airport: Delta and American. Much like Atlanta, DFW runs operations off two sets of parallel runways, north and south, landing on the outside, taking off on the inside.

Airline terminals are in the center of the airport and general aviation is in one corner. DFW has two taxiway bridges that run over the auto access roads to the terminals. There are four bridges; each bridge is one-way and each is numbered by taxiway numbers: "18 bridge." Two ground control frequencies cover the east and west side of the airport, respectively. Frequency changes occur halfway over the bridge.

Flying in or out of DFW is difficult during the summer thunderstorm season, which seems to run from about April through December. Because of traffic volume, the approach and departure controllers blank out weather returns on their scopes. They are aware of where most truly bad weather is and will try to keep you out of it, but will occasionally try to get you to fly too close to a storm.

Remember that ATC is not riding in the aircraft seat and can't feel the bumps. I've seen people take vectors into weather that looked bad just so they wouldn't anger the controller. Remember, it's your rear end and your judgment that will come out during an ensuing NTSB trial if something happens. If it looks very bad don't take the vector, but explain why.

LOS ANGELES INTERNATIONAL AIRPORT:
Approximately 566,000 Annual Operations

For some reason this particular airport seems to have more official arrivals and departures than any other. At last count there were 11 published arrivals and 10 published departures for this single airport.

That is the bad news because it necessitates a lot of study and work to successfully arrive or depart.

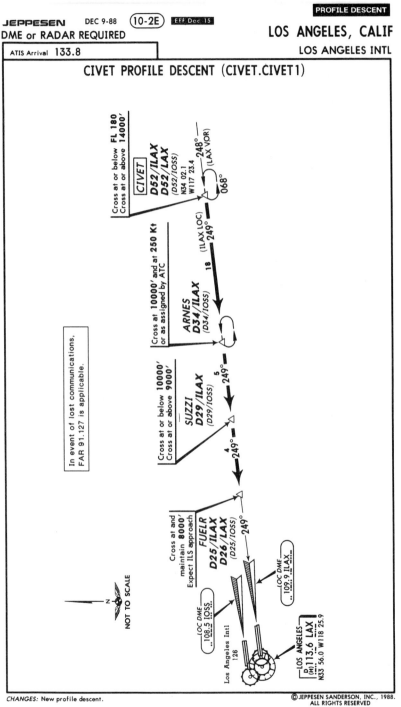

The TWENTYNINE PALMS (CIVETT.CIVET2) arrival. Note the numerous vertical navigation notes and crossing fixes.

An arrival you will face if you plan on landing at Dallas-Ft. Worth International.

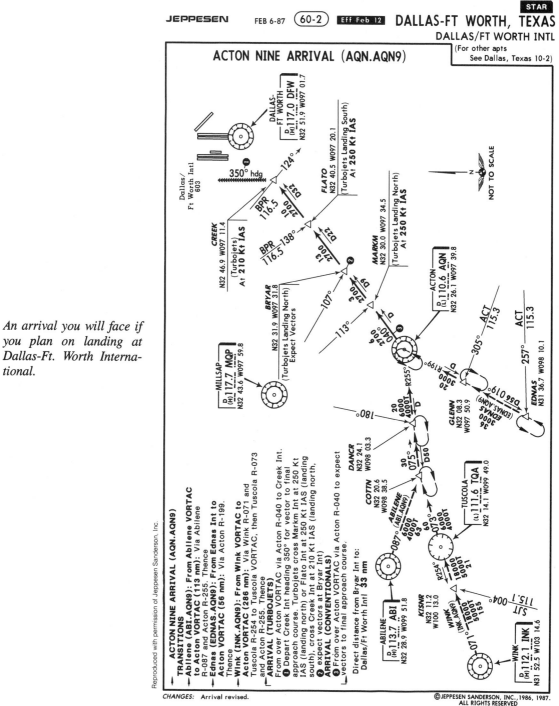

JEPPESEN   FEB 6-87   60-2   Eff Feb 12   **DALLAS-FT WORTH, TEXAS**

STAR

DALLAS/FT WORTH INTL

(For other apts See Dallas, Texas 10-2)

ACTON NINE ARRIVAL (AQN.AQN9)

ACTON NINE ARRIVAL (AQN.AQN9)

TRANSITIONS

Abilene (ABI.AQN9): From Abilene VORTAC to Acton VORTAC (113 nm): Via Abilene R-087 and Acton R-255. Thence

Ednas (EDNAS.AQN9): From Ednas Int to Acton VORTAC (56 nm): Via Acton R-199. Thence

Wink (INK.AQN9): From Wink VORTAC to Acton VORTAC (286 nm): Via Wink R-071 and Tuscola R-254 to Tuscola VORTAC, then Tuscola R-073 and Acton R-255. Thence

ARRIVAL (TURBOJETS)

From over Acton VORTAC via Acton R-040 to Creek Int.
❶ Depart Creek Int heading 350° for vector to final approach course. Turbojets cross Markm Int at 250 Kt IAS (landing north) or Flato Int at 250 Kt IAS (landing south), cross Creek Int at 210 Kt IAS (landing north,
❷ expect vectors at Bryar Int)
ARRIVAL (CONVENTIONALS)
❸ From over Acton VORTAC via Acton R-040 to expect vectors to final approach course.

Direct distance from Bryar Int to:
Dallas/Ft Worth Intl **33 nm**

CHANGES: Arrival revised.

© JEPPESEN SANDERSON, INC., 1986, 1987.
ALL RIGHTS RESERVED

83

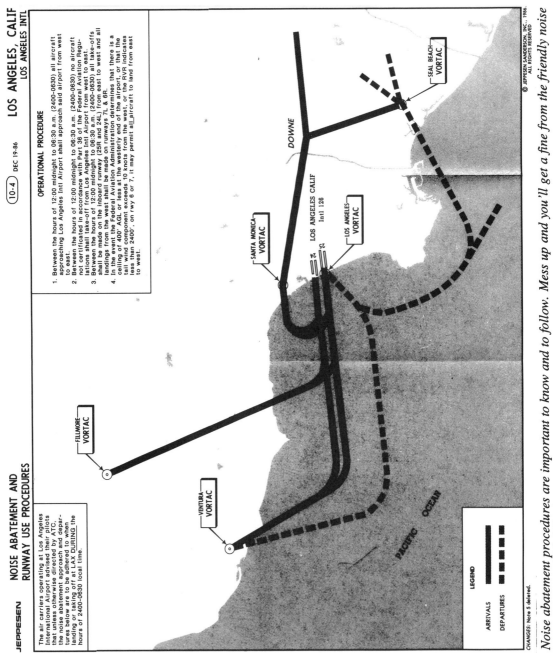

JEPPESEN

NOISE ABATEMENT AND RUNWAY USE PROCEDURES

The air carriers operating at Los Angeles International Airport advised their pilots that unless otherwise directed by ATC, the noise abatement approach and departures below are to be adhered to when landing or taking off at LAX DURING the hours of 2400-0630 local time.

(10-4) DEC 19-86 **LOS ANGELES, CALIF**
LOS ANGELES INTL

OPERATIONAL PROCEDURE

1. Between the hours of 12:00 midnight to 06:30 a.m. (2400-0630) all aircraft approaching Los Angeles Intl Airport shall approach said airport from west to east.
2. Between the hours of 12:00 midnight to 06:30 a.m. (2400-0630) no aircraft not certificated in accordance with Part 36 of the Federal Aviation Regulations shall take-off from Los Angeles Intl Airport from west to east.
3. Between the hours of 12:00 midnight to 06:30 a.m. (2400-0630) all take-offs shall be made on the inboard runway (25R and 24L) from east to west and all landings from the west shall be made on runways 7L & 6R.
4. In the event the Federal Aviation Administration determines that there is a ceiling of 400' AGL or less at the westerly end of the airport, or that the tail wind component exceeds 10 knots from the west, or the RVR indicates less than 2400', on rwy 6 or 7, it may permit all aircraft to land from east to west.

FILLMORE VORTAC

VENTURA VORTAC

SANTA MONICA VORTAC

LOS ANGELES CALIF
Intl 126

LOS ANGELES VORTAC

DOWNE

SEAL BEACH VORTAC

PACIFIC OCEAN

LEGEND

ARRIVALS
DEPARTURES

CHANGES: Note 5 deleted.

© JEPPESEN SANDERSON, INC., 1986.
ALL RIGHTS RESERVED

Noise abatement procedures are important to know and to follow. Mess up and you'll get a fine from the friendly noise monitor. Reproduced with permission of Jeppesen Sanderson, Inc.

The good news is that for the most part, all you have to do is the arrival or departure to operate in this area. If, for example you are planning to land on one of the Runway 25L or 25R, all you would have to do is fly the CIVET.CIVET1 arrival. Everything to make a visual approach to either runway is right there on one chart.

When departing LAX the procedures also help because they don't require much thought while leaving. As long as you follow the departure as cleared, you will have no weird clearances to read, like on the east coast around New York.

Wind at LAX usually comes in off the water, like all other shoreline airports, and you can expect to take off toward the Pacific Ocean most of the time. Keep in mind that their noise abatement and runway-use procedures have you flying quite a bit out over the water before initiating a turn.

Don't forget the taxi chart when flying at LAX. It isn't that complicated but the combination of size and complexity could get you lost pretty quick. Also remember that many of the pilots using this airport speak English only when they are flying and tend to misunderstand the ground controller, too.

MIAMI INTERNATIONAL AIRPORT:
Approximately 350,400 Annual Operations

Language sometimes is also a problem at this airport. Although everyone speaks English, understanding is sometimes difficult.

The TCA is named after Miami International, the primary in this airspace, but it is not necessarily the most difficult airport to fly out of or, for that matter, the busiest in the airspace.

Other airports of note in this TCA are Miami's Opa Locka, and just on the northeast side of the airspace, Fort Lauderdale, Hollywood International. Farther up the beach is Palm Beach International, Boca Raton, and numerous large very busy airports.

Sometimes, especially when operating strictly VFR, the real difficulty lies in making sure you are landing on the correct airport. Most of these airports have parallel east and west runways, have the tower and terminal in the middle of the field, and are all located in urban areas near the beach. More than one pilot has been cleared to land on 9R at Miami International that actually ended up kissing the ground with the mains in Ft. Lauderdale, so be careful.

Miami International presents no huge problems. It is well laid out and it is easy to find your way around.

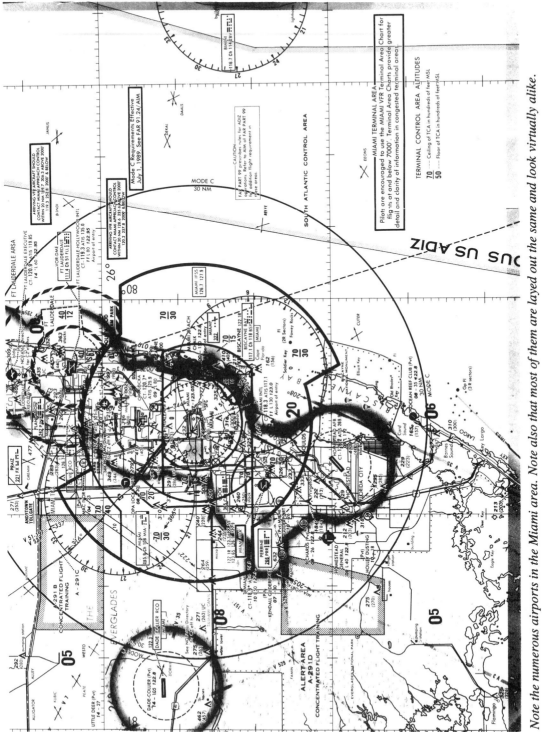

Note the numerous airports in the Miami area. Note also that most of them are layed out the same and look virtually alike.

In south Florida, weather is an ever-present consideration: thunderstorms anytime of year. The controllers are able and willing to help, and with a little care the boomers shouldn't present you with any more problems than usual.

NEW YORK TCA:
Approximately 1,048,000 Annual Operations

The New York TCA actually has three large primary airports: John F. Kennedy International, La Guardia, and Newark International.

Kennedy International is primarily the domain of international airliners. Although served by domestic carriers, they usually just feed the international routes. This makes for some interesting sight-seeing because you get to see aircraft from all over the world.

Aeroflot flies there with the national carriers of Poland, Ireland, China, Australia, and a host of others.

These people are all professional and operate in a world quite different than we are used to. It might be important to keep in mind if you are landing at Kennedy that some of the other people in the traffic pattern might have been in the air for 12 hours or more and are very tired; tired people make mistakes.

Kennedy International has one of the most interesting IFR/VFR approaches around, after the River Visual Approach at Washington's National. The approach at Kennedy is called the "Canarsie" approach by pilots although its official name is the VOR Rwy 13L/R approach.

As you can see from the chart the approach requires flying over the Canarsie VOR and then visually following a series of lights in a curving course to the runway. It is a challenge to locate the correct set of lights because of parallel approaches to both runways (and following a 747 from Thailand in on a rainy night). You have to experience it to believe it.

La Guardia is where domestic airlines hangout. It has 7,000-foot runways perched on the edge of the water on the north side of the city. One of these runways, 4/22, is built on a pier over the water.

Any pilot will tell you that seven thousand feet is long enough for any airplane to land on, but try doing it with a 767 some snowy night. The runway can get very short very fast, especially if you know that running off the end means going for a swim.

La Guardia has a nice general aviation area on the southwest side of the field and, by and large, it is an easy place to navigate while taxiing.

If landing on Runway 22 controllers vector aircraft down the river

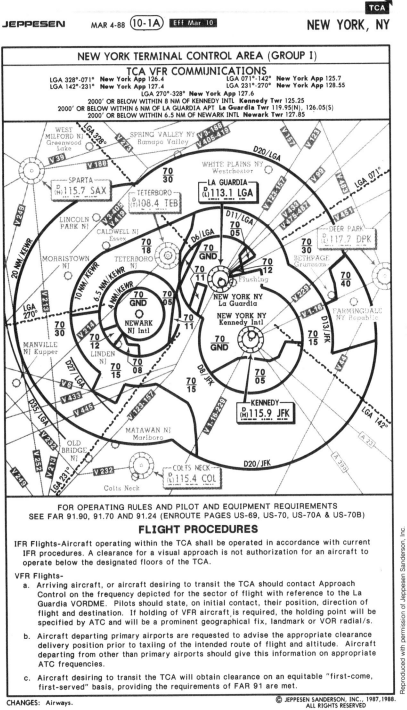

The New York area.

FOR OPERATING RULES AND PILOT AND EQUIPMENT REQUIREMENTS
SEE FAR 91.90, 91.70 AND 91.24 (ENROUTE PAGES US-69, US-70, US-70A & US-70B)

FLIGHT PROCEDURES

IFR Flights-Aircraft operating within the TCA shall be operated in accordance with current IFR procedures. A clearance for a visual approach is not authorization for an aircraft to operate below the designated floors of the TCA.

VFR Flights-

a. Arriving aircraft, or aircraft desiring to transit the TCA should contact Approach Control on the frequency depicted for the sector of flight with reference to the La Guardia VORDME. Pilots should state, on initial contact, their position, direction of flight and destination. If holding of VFR aircraft is required, the holding point will be specified by ATC and will be a prominent geographical fix, landmark or VOR radial/s.

b. Aircraft departing primary airports are requested to advise the appropriate clearance delivery position prior to taxiing of the intended route of flight and altitude. Aircraft departing from other than primary airports should give this information on appropriate ATC frequencies.

c. Aircraft desiring to transit the TCA will obtain clearance on an equitable "first-come, first-served" basis, providing the requirements of FAR 91 are met.

CHANGES: Airways.

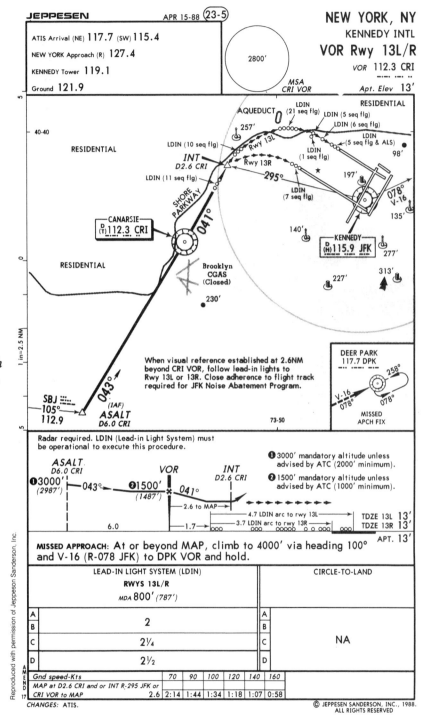

The "Canarsie" approach into Kennedy at New York.

JEPPESEN — APR 15-88 (23-5)

ATIS Arrival (NE) 117.7 (SW) 115.4
NEW YORK Approach (R) 127.4
KENNEDY Tower 119.1
Ground 121.9

NEW YORK, NY
KENNEDY INTL
VOR Rwy 13L/R
VOR 112.3 CRI
Apt. Elev 13'

2800'
MSA CRI VOR

When visual reference established at 2.6NM beyond CRI VOR, follow lead-in lights to Rwy 13L or 13R. Close adherence to flight track required for JFK Noise Abatement Program.

DEER PARK 117.7 DPK — 258° V-16 078° 078° MISSED APCH FIX

Radar required. LDIN (Lead-in Light System) must be operational to execute this procedure.

❶ 3000' mandatory altitude unless advised by ATC (2000' minimum).
❷ 1500' mandatory altitude unless advised by ATC (1000' minimum).

ASALT D6.0 CRI ❶3000' (2987') — 043° — VOR ❷1500' (1487') — 041° — INT D2.6 CRI
2.6 to MAP
6.0 — 1.7
4.7 LDIN arc to rwy 13L — TDZE 13L 13'
3.7 LDIN arc to rwy 13R — TDZE 13R 13'
APT. 13'

MISSED APPROACH: At or beyond MAP, climb to 4000' via heading 100° and V-16 (R-078 JFK) to DPK VOR and hold.

LEAD-IN LIGHT SYSTEM (LDIN) RWYS 13L/R MDA 800' (787')		CIRCLE-TO-LAND
A	2	A
B		B
C	2¼	C
D	2½	D

Circle-to-land: NA

Gnd speed-Kts	70	90	100	120	140	160
MAP at D2.6 CRI and or INT R-295 JFK or CRI VOR to MAP 2.6	2:14	1:44	1:34	1:18	1:07	0:58

CHANGES: ATIS.

giving pilots and passengers a beautiful view of the Statue of Liberty and New York City.

Newark International is probably the least regarded of the three airports and is also the most convenient and least crowded, for pilots and passengers alike. Nice long runways, good approaches, and other good facilities make it a good airport to use for planning business in New York.

The noise abatement procedure is a gentle turn, and although it is a busy airport, the controllers seem in less of a hurry and calmer than the bedlam that might be found at La Guardia.

For an easier time getting into and out of the New York City area I'd suggest using Newark International. It's a little less crowded and not as busy as its other two counterparts and is on the southwest edge of the TCA giving better access if arriving from the south.

SAN FRANCISCO INTERNATIONAL AIRPORT
Approximately 423,000 Annual Operations

San Francisco International Airport was the aerodrome that Robert Stack and John Wayne were trying to reach in that epic movie *The High and The Mighty*, which was the movie that the comedy film *Airplane* was based upon.

The airport is not much like it was described in the movie. It is a very modern, very efficient place that welcomes pilots and aircraft from all over the world. There is quite a mix of domestic and international flights at this field.

As you can see from the taxi chart, there are two sets of parallel runways that meet in the center of the field at just about a 90° angle.

One thing that is in keeping with the movie image and needs to be remembered, especially by VFR pilots, is that hills are located to the northwest of the airport; keep that in mind if departing in that direction. There is terrain above 1,000 ft. MSL roughly three-and-a-half miles to the northwest of the field. SFO field elevation is only 11 feet, so you can see the obvious problem especially if an airplane isn't so hot in the climb department.

San Francisco is well known for foggy weather. The good news is straightforward instrument approaches for IFR types. VFR pilots have numerous airports close by that aren't quite so low and so close to the water, giving a few safe "outs" if the weather at SFO gets scuzzy.

All in all, San Francisco is a nice airport in a great city handled by some of the most professional controllers in the country.

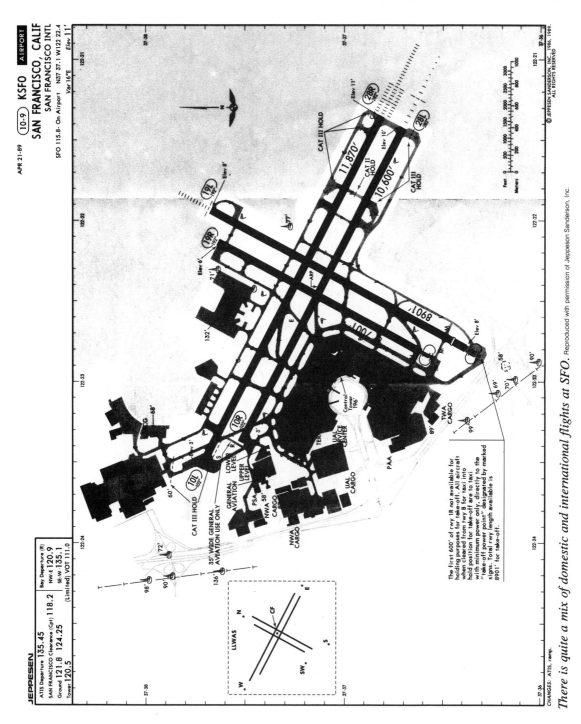

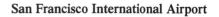

There is quite a mix of domestic and international flights at SFO. Reproduced with permission of Jeppesen Sanderson, Inc.

WASHINGTON NATIONAL AIRPORT:
Fewer than 365,000 Annual Operations

Earlier I mentioned that this airport was considered by many air transport pilots to be one of the scariest and hairiest aerodromes in the United States. That is only partially true. Some pilots will claim that it is by far the absolute scariest airport in the country.

The airport really isn't so bad. It has, as you can see from the chart, three semi-decent runways, the longest is almost 7,000 feet. The airport has a simple taxi-way system and is easy enough to understand how it is laid out.

Now take a step back and notice where the airport is and what location means. The airport is surrounded on three sides by the Potomac river. To the north of the airport notice what is not a restricted area or a warning area, instead see a prohibited area.

This prohibited area is less than three miles from the end of Runway 36. It is not a piece of airspace that means a nasty letter and a slap on the wrist if you fly into it; you might get shot down. During the Vietnam war, a disgruntled person tried to fly a Huey into Richard Nixon's oval office and say "howdy." According to various sources, after that incident the United States Secret Service has *at least* shoulder-fired SAMS at the site, maybe worse. Feeling lucky today?

Actually you would be lucky to lose an engine on a twin after taking off from Runway 36 and made it to the White House to be shot down by people in dark glasses. You would first have to miss the Washington Monument, a small 600-foot-high airplane grabber.

Wind from the south would make a departure much easier . . . .

Check out the River Visual Approach. Looks simple until you realize that this procedure of yanking and banking, places you squeezed between the river and the prohibited areas.

Something not seen on this chart is buildings. I'm not talking about two-story houses, high-rise office buildings all along this river right up to where you make the dramatic right turn, about half-a-mile from the impact point on the runway.

If the description is too complicated, try flying it three miles behind a 727, at night, in the rain or snow. All that's needed is better than a ceiling of 3,500 ft. and more than three miles viz and ATC runs this thing.

If you land a little long because it was a hairy-muffin approach. You start to slide on the runway because it is a little wet or icy and it looks like

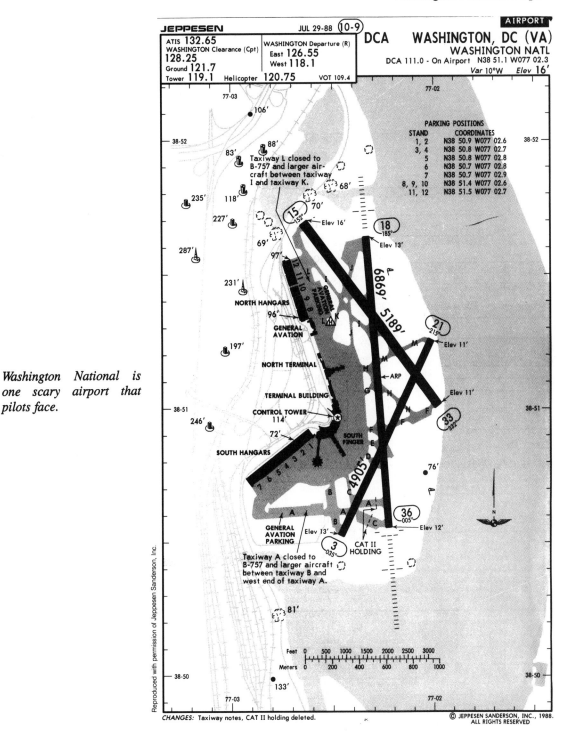

Washington National is one scary airport that pilots face.

JEPPESEN JUL 29-88 (10-9) **AIRPORT**

DCA WASHINGTON, DC (VA)
WASHINGTON NATL
DCA 111.0 - On Airport N38 51.1 W077 02.3
Var 10°W Elev 16'

ATIS 132.65
WASHINGTON Clearance (Cpt) 128.25
Ground 121.7
Tower 119.1 Helicopter 120.75

WASHINGTON Departure (R)
East 126.55
West 118.1
VOT 109.4

PARKING POSITIONS
STAND	COORDINATES
1, 2	N38 50.9 W077 02.6
3, 4	N38 50.8 W077 02.7
5	N38 50.8 W077 02.8
6	N38 50.7 W077 02.8
7	N38 50.7 W077 02.9
8, 9, 10	N38 51.4 W077 02.6
11, 12	N38 51.5 W077 02.7

Taxiway L closed to B-757 and larger aircraft between taxiway I and taxiway K.

Taxiway A closed to B-757 and larger aircraft between taxiway B and west end of taxiway A.

NORTH HANGARS
GENERAL AVIATION
NORTH TERMINAL
TERMINAL BUILDING
CONTROL TOWER 114'
SOUTH HANGARS
SOUTH FINGER
GENERAL AVIATION PARKING
CAT II HOLDING

6869' 5189'
4905'

Feet 0 500 1000 1500 2000 2500 3000
Meters 0 200 400 600 800 1000

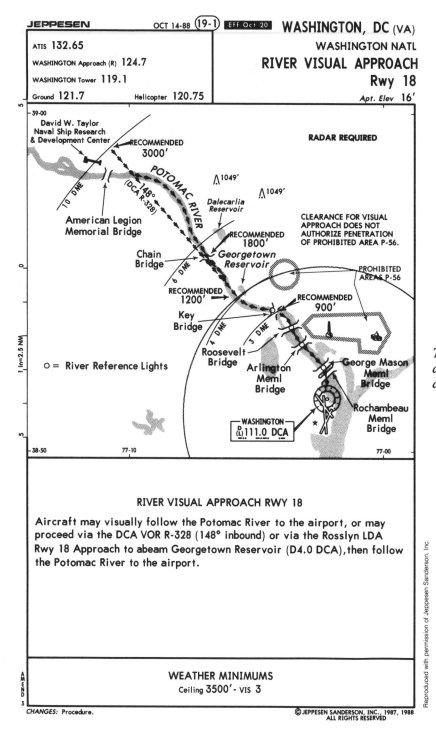

JEPPESEN OCT 14-88 (19-1) Eff Oct 20 **WASHINGTON, DC** (VA)

WASHINGTON NATL
**RIVER VISUAL APPROACH
Rwy 18**

ATIS 132.65

WASHINGTON Approach (R) 124.7

WASHINGTON Tower 119.1

Ground 121.7   Helicopter 120.75

Apt. Elev 16'

RADAR REQUIRED

David W. Taylor
Naval Ship Research
& Development Center

RECOMMENDED
3000'

POTOMAC RIVER

148°
(DCA R-328)

10 DME

1049'

1049'

Dalecarlia
Reservoir

CLEARANCE FOR VISUAL
APPROACH DOES NOT
AUTHORIZE PENETRATION
OF PROHIBITED AREA P-56.

American Legion
Memorial Bridge

RECOMMENDED
1800'

Chain
Bridge

6 DME

Georgetown
Reservoir

PROHIBITED
AREAS P-56

RECOMMENDED
1200'

RECOMMENDED
900'

Key
Bridge

4 DME

3 DME

O = River Reference Lights

Roosevelt
Bridge

Arlington
Meml
Bridge

George Mason
Meml
Bridge

Rochambeau
Meml
Bridge

WASHINGTON
D
(L) 111.0 DCA

*The Washington National
area is rife with restricted
and prohibited areas.*

RIVER VISUAL APPROACH RWY 18

Aircraft may visually follow the Potomac River to the airport, or may
proceed via the DCA VOR R-328 (148° inbound) or via the Rosslyn LDA
Rwy 18 Approach to abeam Georgetown Reservoir (D4.0 DCA), then follow
the Potomac River to the airport.

WEATHER MINIMUMS
Ceiling 3500' - VIS 3

CHANGES: Procedure.

AMEND 3

you'll accidentally run off runway. No problem at most major airports, other than the fact that you'll have a lot of explaining to do . . . . At this one, you're going for a swim. Right after the Air Florida disaster they had a real shortage of rescue boats to pick up the people; how many do they have now?

Pilots are so pumped-up, worrying about whether or not they will safely make the approach or departure, that they pay more attention to operating at National. It is embarrassing as a United States citizen that we, the most powerful nation on earth, have this kind of airport at our capital city.

You've probably figured out by now that large airports are not that bad. Just make sure you're prepared and large airports should not present problems that you can't handle.

7
Safety Techniques: VFR

EVEN THOUGH FLYING IN THIS COUNTRY IS NOWADAYS CONSIDERED to be a very technical, gizmo-oriented task, the fact remains that collision avoidance is still predicated on a "seen-and-be-seen" concept.

You might be flying the latest technology in a Boeing 767, using the FMS (flight management system), the autopilot, and automatic throttles. When traffic arises on the controller's scope, he will still call it out in the form of a visual reference to an analog clock face: "Traffic two o'clock, a mile-and-a-half, altitude unknown."

Unless technology drastically changes, a pilot will still be expected to use the oldest of all known collision avoidance devices, his eyes.

EYES

Let's not put down these ancient scanning devices. Nothing can or will ever compare to eyes when it comes to detecting, judging, and avoiding other aircraft in crowded skies.

Eyes can pick out objects hundreds and thousands of light-years away. When was last time you looked up in the sky at the stars? They can also pick out the smallest of details when focused on close range. This is not a "Mister Wizard" lecture. I just want you to realize that in the box of survival tools in congested airspace, eyes are the most important.

Like all tools, eyes are prone to error and misuse. If you have a weather radar on board and don't know how to properly use it, or aren't aware of built-in errors, you are probably better off not using it. It is the same thing with the more "organic" tools: eyes.

One trait of eyes is that in order for them to see something properly they must be looking directly at the object in question. You certainly might see that aircraft approaching from the side using peripheral vision, but distance and direction might be hard to determine.

Images moving across your field of vision are very hard to see correctly and almost impossible to judge. For that reason a quick scan for traffic using fast head movements is pretty much a waste of time. You will either miss the traffic completely or misjudge it.

It is true that an eye can scan 200° range in a glance. The problem that arises is that an eye only has a very small part of the retina, in the center, called the "fovea" that has the ability to send sharp, focused images to the brain. All other information that is not processed by the fovea will be less detailed and clear to the brain in its interpretation of the data. For example, an aircraft that is seven miles away and observed by the fovea would have to be $7/10$ of a mile away for the brain to recognize it.

Look around for traffic in small, regularly spaced eye movements.

According to the FAA, the best way to scan outside an aircraft is to take it in short, regularly spaced eye movements that bring areas of the sky, one after the other, into a central visual field. FAA recommends that each eye movement should be limited to about 10° and each area should be observed for at least one second for a better chance to see something.

Most experts recommend that a scan outside the aircraft using a "sectors" method. Look at one section of the sky at a time, letting the eyes focus on just that sector. Try to work out a personal pattern that will allow you to make a complete scan of the sky on a regular basis, but still allows enough time for the eyes to get the whole picture.

HOW LONG?

Just about every pilot and aviation book agrees that everybody should spend a lot of time looking out of the cockpit searching for traffic. From the very first flying lesson, pilots are taught to "keep the neck on a swivel" and point out to the instructor any airplanes they might see, even if they think the instructor already sees them.

Let's face it, flying an aircraft today, especially in such airspace as a TCA or ARSA, requires a certain amount of precision. You are required to maintain certain altitudes and headings even if you are a VFR-only pilot. Monitoring instruments will require eyes in the cockpit more than usual, at a time when you are operating around a lot of traffic.

This is becoming especially true of the newer airliners present in crowded airspace. Although they do have great new autopilots and automatic flight systems of all types, the point remains that they must be programmed. The programming keypads are, you guessed it, located inside the cockpit in a place where one or more of the pilots must look down and concentrate on punching in the correct data.

Although heads-up displays (HUDs) are currently in use in certain military aircraft, and are on the horizon for airliners and general aviation aircraft, for the time being everytime you want to see what the aircraft is doing you must shift attention and eyesight back into the airplane.

FAA studies have shown that the time most pilots spend looking inside the cockpit *should* represent roughly $1/3$ to $1/4$ of the scan time outside the aircraft, with four or five seconds spent looking inside.

I would guess that the FAA studies are a little out of whack with the way most pilots operate in the real world. I know I have been guilty of spending long periods of time staring at the instruments, especially in nice VFR weather, and suspect most pilots do the same. While it will probably drive you crazy to figure out what percentage of time is spent peering at the outside world, it is a good idea to work on spending as much eyeball time as possible looking for other aircraft.

GOOD SCANNING

Most people are comfortable looking from left to right, so it is probably a good idea to get in the habit of starting a scan on the left shoulder and working to the right. Take the field of vision a little bit at a time and take a little time to let the eyes focus .

If you take a quick look outside (at a single 10° area) and then look quickly inside at the instruments, your eyes will probably tire quicker. Make a larger outside scan first.

The important thing about all this talk of scanning is to do what works best for you. You can get a bad headache just thinking about scanning techniques. Be aware that especially in crowded airspace, your eyes are your life.

NIGHT VISION

When it is dark outside a pilot faces additional "eye errors" and must deal with them in order to enhance safety.

Obviously, unless other aircraft are sporting very visible lighting such as strobes, landing light, or logo lights, you will have a more difficult time seeing them at night. Another problem is that it is harder for eyes to judge distance and direction at night. If you see aircraft navigation lights, green on the left and red on the right, is it going away from you or heading right at you?

Takes a minute to figure out, doesn't it? In the air, if it is heading right at you—and in this case, it is—you might not have enough time to try to remember that the green navigation light is always mounted on the right wing.

Aircraft lights can cause many illusions. It is not uncommon at night to think you are on a collision course with another aircraft only to find out that it is six miles away.

Small print, colors on charts, and aircraft instruments are more difficult to see during dim conditions. Without adequate cockpit lighting, seeing things in the aircraft is impossible, but it creates another vision problem: dark adaptation.

Dark adaptation is the reason that many aircraft still have red instrument lights. In order for the eye to adapt to dim lighting outside, it takes up to 30 minutes of complete darkness. Most pilots can achieve some degree of "night vision" after 20 minutes exposed to only very dim red instrument lights.

This was valuable when flying at night in World War II, but has very little value in terms of safety in the night skies of the 1990s. As a matter of fact using only red instrument lighting has drawbacks that you can't properly read charts and instruments and might lead to disorientation, something you definitely don't want while flying.

Like most other things in flying and life, you have to achieve some form of balance. Keep the instrument lights dim enough to maximize outside vision, but bright enough to read the instruments and fly the aircraft.

EMPTY FIELD MYOPIA

Eyes are great instruments. They automatically go into a form of automatic "relaxation mode" when nothing is to be seen.

Flying VFR above an overcast, or a large body of water, there is nothing specific for the eyes to examine. Eyes will automatically relax and adjust to a comfortable focal distance of 10 to 30 feet. This is extremely bad news. In other words, the pop-up traffic that is headed straight at you might not enter focused eyesight or thoughts until it is 10 to 30 feet away . . ..

Combat "autolaziness" with an active scan. Try to keep the eyes moving around the cockpit and outside the aircraft. The habit of just staring at the horizon over the glare shield might make you guilty of looking without seeing.

VFR COLLISION AVOIDANCE

Let's say that you are flying along and you see another aircraft out ahead. Congratulations, you have just successfully made the first step toward survival. If you can see it, you have a much, much better chance of missing it, even if ATC has advised. You might not be looking at the traffic ATC mentioned and you might never see the one that hits you.

How can you tell if you are on a collision course with traffic?

Determining relative altitude means that if the traffic in question appears to be below the horizon, it is probably below you. If it is above the horizon it is probably above you, and if it is right on the horizon it is probably at the same altitude.

I think you can already see the problem with this one. Just one glance at the approaching traffic might provide the false impression of safety. Let's say that traffic appears well below or above the horizon. One major attraction for aircraft is that they can climb and descend. An aircraft that is above the horizon and descending might mean serious trouble.

Unfortunately there is no way to determine if the other airplane is climbing or descending, unless watched to notice its movement relative to the horizon. That sounds good too, but in the real world more than that one aircraft might be out there. Other traffic might be called out by ATC, you will be busy flying the airplane, and, if flying in a TCA, you will be expected to fly with a relative degree of accuracy, which means more instrument scanning even when VFR.

COLLISION POSSIBILITIES

An old rule in collision avoidance goes something like this: "If it stays in one spot on the windshield, it is a collision course."

This little maxim is true, pretty much. Remember learning spot landings and the instructor explaining to put the spot in the windshield and keeping it there to ensure landing on the mark.

Rest assured, that if another aircraft is staying in the same spot on the windshield, and it is getting larger, that means serious trouble, get out of there.

It might be difficult to see the most threatening aircraft, one that isn't moving on the windscreen or field of vision for the reasons we went over earlier in the chapter. Your eye will tend to ignore a stationary target because it prefers to track a moving target. Unless the target is directly in the center of line of sight, the eye might ignore it completely until very, very close.

EVASIVE ACTION

The FAA, in its recommendations, suggests remembering the right-of-way rules and trying to follow applicable FARs to avoid another aircraft.

This is nice and I am sure it is reassuring to people in quiet, air conditioned offices, with plenty of time to think things out in a rational manner.

You don't have that luxury. You are mere seconds away from an accident. The best way to avoid colliding with that other aircraft is anyway you possibly can.

Think about it while reading this: in the air, surprised to discover an Aztec appearing in the lower left corner of the windshield and getting larger; your mind will have only about a second to register. If you are flying a light twin the closure rate is probably somewhere around 360 knots.

If you noticed this traffic when it was a quarter-mile away, that means you have only approximately 2.5 seconds. Figure that it takes an airplane roughly a second to react to input, especially if flying on autopilot. That leaves a second-and-a-half to decide how to avoid a collision.

This one-and-a-half second interval will probably not be long enough for a brain to look up the pertinent FARs and right-of-way rules. You will be depending mostly on reflex action in this case and the nervous system will take over and make you fly away from the threat. Please don't train to try and remember regulations in situations like this. I would rather have you explain to the FAA and NTSB about the decision than to have some government official deal with the alternative.

OVERSTRESSING AN AIRCRAFT

Nothing overstresses an airplane like a midair collision. Your body will probably tell if the yanking and banking is too much to avoid the threat. Most potential accidents like this don't require a huge correction for avoidance. Don't be surprised, though, if the nervous system makes you take a big correction.

Obviously, yanking an aircraft into an aerobatic maneuver that you can't recover from is probably not a huge improvement over a midair but most likely you won't allow it. And if it is necessary to perform a radical maneuver to avoid an accident, that is much better.

MULTIPLE THREATS

One of the first things to consider when spotting traffic is the fact that other airplanes are out there.

It won't do much good to avoid one aircraft only to blunder into another that you weren't thinking about. This is especially true in congested environments like traffic patterns. A little awareness of where you are and what you are trying to do will go a long way.

For example, when flying the visual approach to Runway 8R in Atlanta, traffic pulls in front and you would know that it would be much safer to break right than to break left. Because aircraft are shooting parallel approaches to your left! It won't do much good to avoid one conflict, only to fight 10 others.

CLEARING TURNS

Anybody that has taken one flying lesson is familiar with the concept of "clearing turns." A good instructor stressed from the very first day the importance of avoiding collisions.

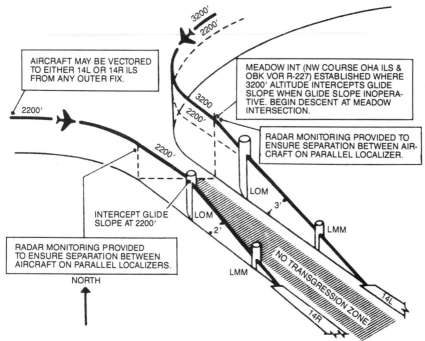

AIRCRAFT MAY BE VECTORED TO EITHER 14L OR 14R ILS FROM ANY OUTER FIX.

MEADOW INT (NW COURSE OHA ILS & OBK VOR R-227) ESTABLISHED WHERE 3200' ALTITUDE INTERCEPTS GLIDE SLOPE WHEN GLIDE SLOPE INOPERATIVE. BEGIN DESCENT AT MEADOW INTERSECTION.

RADAR MONITORING PROVIDED TO ENSURE SEPARATION BETWEEN AIRCRAFT ON PARALLEL LOCALIZER.

INTERCEPT GLIDE SLOPE AT 2200'

RADAR MONITORING PROVIDED TO ENSURE SEPARATION BETWEEN AIRCRAFT ON PARALLEL LOCALIZERS.

NORTH

During parallel approaches always perform a missed approach to the opposite side of the parallel traffic.

You were taught to make a series of two clearing turns of at least a 90° heading change, one to the left and then one to the right, before a maneuver. This was done to make sure that the area was clear.

Making 90° turns won't hack it in a TCA environment like New York's, but you still can look under or over that wing before you start that heading change that ATC requested. It doesn't take much. On a high-wing airplane, just lift the wing on the turning side a few degrees and peek under it. This is also a good time to glance in the direction away from the turn also. If you are VFR in a very congested piece of airspace chances are that everybody is flying faster than you. That airplane you're turning away from might be closing in at more than 200 knots.

Be sure, once again, while making these turns to look both above and below the aircraft. Remember, aircraft can climb and descend and do not have to be level with you to be a threat.

COCKPIT MANAGEMENT

It is pretty clear to just about everyone that if a cockpit is neat and tidy and the pilot can put hands on any necessary information, like charts and checklists, that you will have more time to look outside the aircraft.

There are many ways you can manage to clean up the act. Prior planning is important. Log necessary radio frequencies and attach the list to a knee-board or pad on the yoke. If using some form of arrival or local chart, place it either on your lap aligned to the direction of flight, or at least have it in hand without searching all over the cockpit.

Nothing is more time consuming and wasteful than looking in vain for an ATIS or approach control frequency while trying to fly the airplane and avoid that DC-3 that just popped up in the windshield. Keep all radio frequencies handy and in order for more time looking out the windows.

Learn about a new area. This would include the VORs, landmarks ATC might request that you fly around and where other airports are to avoid traffic patterns, arrivals, and departures.

CONGESTED AREAS

Because most airplanes still navigate by reference to VORs, a lot of traffic will cross directly over them. Keep firmly in mind that even though you are flying VFR, many IFR flights might be cleared over the same fix. For example, Rome, Georgia, is one of the primary fixes on the arrival pattern at Atlanta's Hartsfield International Airport. Almost every bit of traffic flowing into Hartsfield from the northeast flies over this VOR. You are perfectly within right to fly VFR over this fix at any legal VFR cruise altitude. The VOR lies outside the Atlanta TCA and you don't even have to be in radio contact with ATC or have a transponder to fly in the area.

It is a fact of life, though, that turbojets will be flying over Rome VOR, five miles in trail, at about 13,000 ft. MSL by the dozens at any given time of day. The minimum en route altitude for the Rome Arrival is 4,000 ft. MSL, so it wouldn't be surprising to see dozens of general aviation aircraft coming over this fix, too.

You can see that even if you weren't going to have anything to do that day with Atlanta—a flight from Chattanooga to Montgomery—you still might find a world of trouble in terms of traffic when near Rome VOR.

Even if you are planning to land at Hartsfield, in radar contact with ATC, and doing everything they request, you are still in greater danger over a heavily traveled fix like Rome because, as we saw earlier, VFR pilots may operate over this VOR any time they like, at any legal altitude they like and might not be on radar.

Many other places besides VORs require caution. A good example would be Miami, Florida, just west of Fort Lauderdale, West Palm Beach, and Boca Raton. If you fly in this area you are probably familiar with the "canal," a large north and south drainage ditch just west of the city and Interstate 75 and the Florida Turnpike.

West of this line lies the Everglades, to the east, some of the busiest airports in the south. Most local VFR pilots in the area know that if they stay west of that line, they are going to be free of the heavy traffic going into Miami International and Fort Lauderdale. The traffic for these airports does usually come from the west because the prevailing wind is usu-

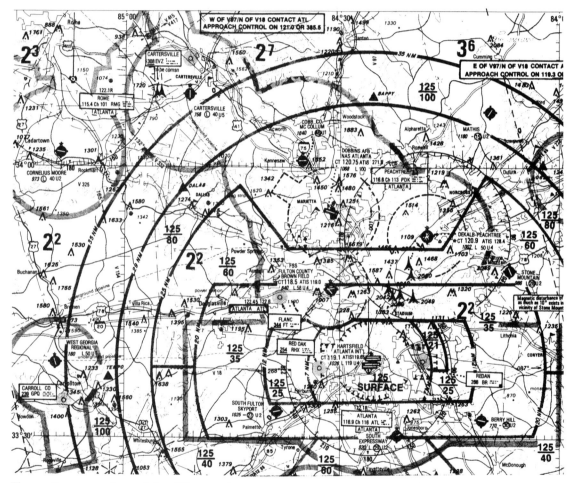

The northwest quadrant of the ATL area chart.

The Rome arrival into Atlanta might be crowded with VFR traffic not controlled by ATC.

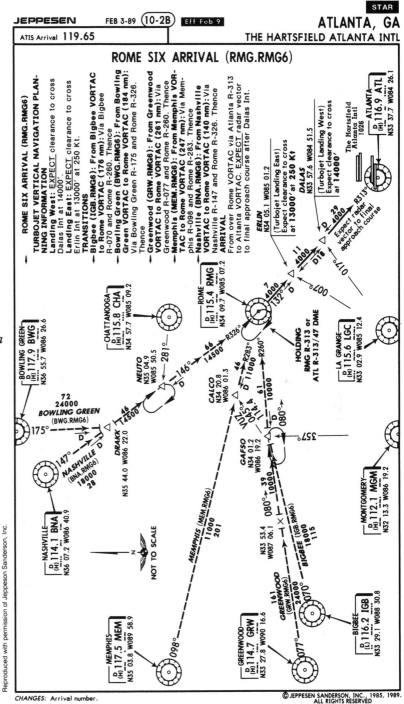

107

ally from the east, but they almost always cross this canal at 3,000 ft. MSL or above. If you wandered a few miles east of this line and tried to fly VFR north or south you would be covered by 727s, DC-9s, and L-1011s.

MAKE IT EASIER

Some of the most effective techniques available are the simplest:

- A CLEAN WINDSHIELD. Is that an F-16 coming right at you or is it a bug you hit on final two weeks ago? Sounds unnecessary, but you can save many frightening experiences by cleaning the windshield from time to time.
- DON'T BLOCK YOUR VISION. There are enough natural obstructions to vision, like doorposts, struts, wings, and engines without adding to them.

  No problem if you want to stack charts on the glareshield for a minute, but don't leave them there all day. Same thing goes for hats, coffee cups, aircraft curtains, and a Cabbage Patch doll!

  If it is between your eyes and the windshield or window, it is in your way and is a potential safety hazard.
- LIGHTS. Even in broad daylight, your landing lights can save your life. Any exterior light can be used to become more visible to other pilots any time of the day. Navigational lights might be just the thing that catches the other pilot's eye that's on a collision course with you.

  Definitely use all the lights that are available: strobes, the rotating beacon, navigational lights, logo lights, anti-ice lights, taxi lights (if your gear is down), and especially landing lights.

  Most airline pilots and other pilots of large aircraft use all landing lights any time they are below 10,000 ft. MSL, no matter the time of day. It makes the aircraft 10 times more visible to other pilots. There is no reason why this technique shouldn't work on all aircraft, especially those that are smaller or might not have strobes. Everything that can make you more visible to the other pilot might save your life.
- UTILIZE LABOR SAVING DEVICES. Yeah, I know it's not cool to use an autopilot all the time, especially when trying to impress

passengers with flying skills. The autopilot and other labor saving devices could save your life because they free your mind for the all-important chore of traffic avoidance.

It has already been mentioned that it is a pain to face the fact that when you should be looking outside the aircraft, the more you are required by ATC and the FARs to fly the airplane more precisely in terms of heading and altitude. If you have an autopilot that will hold altitude or even just a heading while you peer outside, that will allow much more time to search for traffic, instead of staring at the altimeter or heading indicator.

When entering congested airspace, leave your ego at home. If there is a tool or piece of equipment on board that will help do the job easier and safer, use it. Next, let's talk about one of the best, and least-used VFR tools any aircraft can carry.

- PASSENGERS. Unless you are flying an airliner or a big corporate jet, you are probably in close contact with the passengers. Passengers have eyes too, why not use them?

  There is no need to scare everybody on board with horror stories. As you make the usual pre-takeoff briefing about seat belts and emergency exits, include this: "If any of you see any other aircraft around us while we're flying, be sure to quietly point them out to me, even if you think I already see them."

  Passengers will probably be looking out the windows anyway. Use those extra eyes to enhance safety. You have to ask them though because many passengers think that you already see the traffic or you will get mad at them if they mention it.

OUT-FAKE THE WAKE

If it hasn't happened yet, it is bound to sooner or later around large, crowded airports. You will find yourself on final approach some fine day and the controller will say: "Piper two-seven alpha, cleared to land runway two-six right, wind calm, caution wake turbulence, Boeing 767 five miles ahead landing."

You will most likely feel a large bump and then the world will try to turn upside-down.

This isn't just a problem for general aviation pilots. I've been in DC-9s and 727s that have gone through some very interesting rolling maneuvers behind heavies.

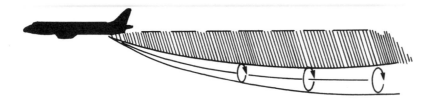

Knowledge and planning can help you ''outfake'' the wake.

If you are flying a light airplane remember that everything bigger is a heavy. The FAA only technically recognizes aircraft that have a certificated gross weight of more than 300,000 pounds as a heavy. Although ATC will usually warn about the others they aren't under the same onus to provide spacing on them for you.

A fully grossed-out Boeing 727 can weigh more than 182,500 pounds; a DC-9 can weigh more than 100,000 pounds. Just about any airliner, jet or transport, can cause serious problems.

A little thought of, but catastrophic, form of wake turbulence comes from helicopters. You don't expect such a small aircraft to cause much problem, but try landing or taxiing by one that is near the ground in a hover.

A few things to remember:

1. Wake turbulence can kill. If you get in the wing tip vortice of a large aircraft, you might experience a roll rate of more than 720° per second. That's twice the maximum roll rate of most production aircraft.
2. Wake turbulence can hang around. Although the vortices do sink, they do so slowly in calm air. Also, if there is a crosswind, the turbulence can blow over from a parallel runway.
3. If you can, fly above the flight path of the "heavy" to avoid the turbulence. This is easy on landing, especially if the airplane is equipped with an ILS receiver and the runway has that approach. If there is a glideslope available to a runway, the airlines are required by FARs to be on or above the glideslope. They'll usually be on it, so the safety factor should be to stay above it. This will put you above the wake. You will land a bit long if you do this, but you are in a light aircraft and the runway was long enough to land the heavy, the runway is probably very long.

On takeoff you will have a problem because it is very unlikely you will be able to climb better than something like a Boeing 767. In this case ATC will make you wait either two minutes or until the heavy is at least five miles away when you leave the ground. Remember that ATC will not provide separation from a 727 or DC-9 unless you ask for it.

Asking for more time behind a heavy is no crime. The controllers would usually rather see you cause a short delay rather than become involved in an accident. At the larger airports, ATC will probably allow a departure from an intersection. If you think you want more time, just ask for it because ATC can't make you take off if you don't want to.

Along with the usual cautions about landing and taking off around heavies, be careful about crossing their wakes. You can get quite a jolt, although they're not life threatening like flying directly behind one in the same direction.

If you become entangled in the clutches of wake turbulence, it is important to treat it like an emergency because it is. Get out of there. If on a short final, it is unlikely you will complete the landing anyway, so go around. In any case, get out of it the best way possible. You will have a feeling about this, so lecturing here won't help much. If you are on final, you can probably climb out of it, it is doubtful you can do that on takeoff. The best thing is to turn out of it as soon as possible keeping in mind that there might be a lot of other traffic present. Don't press your luck with wake turbulence. It can kill you.

GOVERNMENT ASSISTANCE

This is your big chance to recoup some of that tax money you've been "donating" over the years to the federal government!

When you are flying VFR in any airspace, anywhere in the United States, there are literally thousands of highly trained government employees eager to help. The company they work for is called the FAA. They are called air traffic controllers and flight service station specialists.

You already know that when operating an aircraft in either an ARSA or TCA that you are required to at least be in radio contact with ATC. You should also know that many other instances exist when ATC will provide vectors and traffic advisories: ask.

VFR Flight Following

On a work load permitting basis, a VFR pilot has access to any FAA radar facility in this country.

You are already familiar with the services available in such airspace as TRSAs, ARSAs and TCAs. Some of this "service" is mandatory type; TCAs and ARSAs require radio contact with ATC.

Many times, practically the same service available in these areas is still available in the more mundane airspace that an en route center controls.

If flying through the Atlanta area, make good use of the VFR traffic advisories that might be available from center. Not only would contact be beneficial to you, center would also benefit because you would no longer be the "VFR traffic, altitude unknown" called out to IFR traffic and other VFR traffic. They would know you and would also know altitude and intentions.

You should be able to get some form of VFR flight following or VFR traffic advisories anytime the controller has time available. This service is based upon "work load permitting."

Work load Permitting

This is a paradox. When the controller has enough time to work with people that request VFR flight following, or VFR traffic advisories, it usually means there really isn't that much traffic to worry about. When the controller is way too busy to work you and advises "Unable to work you at this time. Please squawk 1200, frequency change approved," that usually means that the skies are so full of aircraft that ATC can't spare a few seconds.

Determine if the controller's work load will permit your aircraft by asking. On the initial call up, the controller will either issue a discreet transponder code or say that he's too busy.

A variety of sources provide the proper frequency to contact ATC to get VFR service. First would be a sectional chart if close to a TCA. The frequencies are listed on the chart next to the TCA.

Other places that might offer a usable frequency would be the *Airman's Information Manual*, many airport guides, any Jeppesen IFR en route chart, or NOS charts. On Jeppesen en route charts, center frequencies are all listed on the back.

IFR charts for VFR use? No, I don't recommend using instrument charts if you are a VFR-only pilot. Too many landmarks and details will be missed if you rely on instrument charts for VFR navigation. IFR charts are handy to have when trying to find an airway or a center frequency.

As a matter of fact, many IFR pilots carry VFR charts in addition to IFR charts to pick out landmarks not depicted on the IFR charts.

If you are instrument rated, current, qualified, and flying a suitably equipped aircraft into congested airspace like TCAs, you are probably better off filing IFR and using the system prepared for IFR operators. You will save a lot of time and hassle getting in and out of these places.

If you are not to be instrument rated, never wanted to be, and have no desire to become rated, there is absolutely nothing wrong. Flying an aircraft under visual flight rules with skill, whether in congested airspace or not, is becoming a dying art. Many VFR-only pilots that I have had the honor to fly with are "twice the pilot" compared to selected "gauge gazers," that I've encountered.

Over all, the important thing when flying VFR in crowded airspace is to come out of it successfully and intact. Anything else is just window dressing.

8
Safety Techniques: IFR

SO, YOU HAVE IT MADE. YOU ARE WELL BEYOND THAT PERIOD OF LIFE when overcast skies and reduced visibility could ruin your whole flying day. You have paid your dues, not to mention the copious amounts of money paid for training for the rating.

Smartly at the controls of a fast single-engine retractable or light twin, you are surrounded with the best in avionics and instrumentation.

No longer slave to the whims of the weather you may proudly and legally ply the crowded skies of any terminal control area or other crowded parcel of airspace in the country. No more uncertainty about that shopping mall you are circling at ATC's request because you can pinpoint your position within a cat's whisker on an ultramodern package of navigation do-dads.

You are on your way, do-dads and all, with business partners to drop them off at O'Hare to connect with a JAL flight to Tokyo. The weather is clear and smooth and you can make out the shape of Lake Michigan as you approach Boiler VOR from the south. The controller's voice interrupts:

"Piper three five six four six I have a clearance for you when you are ready to copy."

"Piper six four six I have an amended clearance when you're ready to copy."

You snap out a fresh sheet of paper on the state-of-the-art knee-board and say: "Yeah, go ahead center."

"Piper three five six four six is cleared to the Chicago Heights VOR, hold south on the 190 degree radial, right turns, ten mile legs approved. Expect further clearance at two three five five, time now two three zero five."

Well, at least the entry will be an easy direct type, but a 50-minute hold on a clear day is unpleasant.

In terms of problems faced as an IFR pilot in a crowded environment, the one above is the easiest. All you have to worry about is:

1. Fuel status (you planned for an hour-and-a-half hold time plus reserves).

2. Passengers' schedule (their flight to Tokyo leaves in an hour).
3. Flying the aircraft precisely enough to avoid hitting any of the other six airplanes holding over the Heights.

The same problems would occur when flying into O'Hare VFR. The precision part wouldn't be as important. Realize that just because of those gadgets and the skill to use them, it doesn't mean all will be smooth and hassle free.

A COMMON STRATEGY

Safety and a happy life in the big leagues of flying with the jet-set relies on the same basics discussed in the VFR chapter. Once again the best tools in the safety tool chest are eyes.

Eyes are going to be preoccupied with minding the store in the cockpit when flying IFR, especially in actual instrument conditions. The whole point of instrument flying is supposed to be flying the aircraft by reference to instruments only.

While being "in the soup" technically relieves a pilot of worrying about dodging VFR-only traffic, this attitude can lead to serious trouble.

It might be the first faulty assumption you have made, especially since you always follow the FARs and wouldn't think of flying through clouds unless without an ATC clearance; some people out there illegally fly through clouds and TCAs without clearances everyday.

Assuming that traffic is in the clouds with you, and also assuming the controller doesn't see the offending aircraft on radar to call it out, what makes you think that traffic is visible in clouds?

Interesting point isn't it, which leads to a question regarding visibility in clouds.

Think about it for a minute. Cruising in a solid cloud bank at 6,000 ft. MSL. Wing tips are visible without distortion. How much farther can you see in this cloud? You're surrounded by whiteness but are you actually still in the cloud? Could you just be in between two indistinct layers?

The point is, you don't know because no frame of reference exists. You might think you can see two feet in front of the windshield, but might actually have 3/4 of a mile visibility: no way of knowing unless a physical object is out there, such as another aircraft.

The discussion of "empty field myopia" in the previous chapter comes to mind. If ever there was a case for this, it is here in the clouds. Not only are you conditioned as a pilot not to peer out of the windows when you think you are in the clouds, eyes also conspire to rob you of observation talents when needed most.

There have been many occasions in my flying life when I was IMC (instrument meteorological conditions), thought I was all by myself enclosed by clouds and still saw other aircraft cruise by at least a thousand feet away vertically. As a matter of fact, this happens all the time in situations like the holding pattern described earlier. The point is, you just don't know how much you can see unless you look out of the windows.

It isn't easy to do this outside observing because training as an instrument pilot has negated most of the "keep your head on a swivel" training as a pre-solo student.

When you flew with a hood during instrument training and you raised your head the instructor might slam it with a rolled-up chart and yell "No cheating!" Well, it had its place when the intent was to keep you from figuring out if you were blue side up by looking outside, but that swat was another, more tacit lesson: real instrument pilots don't look outside of the aircraft, even for a moment.

The second and more sobering lesson you learned was that in the clouds, if you looked outside too long, when you looked in, you were disoriented. Staring outside too long in actual conditions can yield a 30° bank without trying.

These two lessons that have been reinforced by years of trying to keep altitude and heading and course right on the money have probably led to the habit of not looking outside very often when operating IFR.

This habit can be very dangerous. Not only will people fly through cloudy weather without a clearance, or any contact with ATC, perfectly legal pilots operating in a legal manner can be a problem.

Most of the time when operating an aircraft on an IFR clearance in congested airspace, the weather is at least basic VFR. Although you did get the instrument rating to fly through just about any kind of weather, for the majority of the time you fly VFR on an IFR clearance.

Unless flying above Flight Level 180 and operating in positive control airspace, you will have to face the fact that you are sharing the skies with VFR pilots that might or might not be in any contact with ATC.

Also, unless flying above 12,500 ft.MSL, even if the controller points out traffic as you fly in and out of the clouds, it is unlikely you will get any altitude information. Remember, above 12,500 ft., aircraft are required by regulation to be equipped with an operating Mode C transponder.

Sometimes the "mix" can get pretty hairy. Even if everyone is following the FARs to the letter, "close calls" can occur.

Let's say you are flying along dumb and happy at 12,000 ft. on an IFR clearance. You are flying on the centerline of the airway, exactly on altitude, and have been listening to the melodic voice of the controller as he talks to other traffic. You are flying in and out of a broken overcast that starts at about 11,800 ft.

Suddenly you see another aircraft headed right for you! It is a DC-3, it is huge, and it is headed right for you. What should you do? Of course, you maneuver the aircraft to avoid the collision.

Of course, you weren't really going to collide with that DC-3. It was also operating perfect legally. The pilot of the Douglas in question was following the applicable FARs to the letter. The weather was nice, so he decided that filing IFR would be a hassle. He decided to fly airways back to the home base and chose to cruise at a VFR cruising altitude of 11,500 ft. MSL which was perfectly legal for his direction of flight.

Although he probably should have been talking to ATC just as a precaution, he decided, quite properly, not to. All the controller could see on his scope that might have helped you avoid this scare was a VFR transponder code return of 1200. Normally ATC would have called this out to you, but the work load was heavy at the moment, so he didn't, nor was he required to do so.

Popping out of that cloud an eighth of a mile from the oncoming DC-3, you reacted properly: the nervous system's classical "flight response."

Although ATC is required to point out traffic to the IFR pilot, when you are operating in TCAs and ARSAs, ATC's definition of pertinent traffic will usually vary with their work load.

If there is no apparent conflict they might fail to tell anything about traffic that you might consider a threat.

The only way to protect yourself when flying IFR during VFR conditions, is to keep the eyes open and outside the cockpit as if flying VFR. Remember, ATC is only charged with separating you from other IFR traffic when you are flying on an IFR clearance. They will try to point out VFR traffic, but you are really on your own.

IFR FLYING STRATEGIES

Many of the same survival strategies you used as a VFR pilot are equally important in the clouds. We'll review all of them later in the chapter. The important thing to keep in mind when flying IFR in complex, congested airspace is to keep it simple and stick to the basics.

Keeping it simple isn't all that easy. The main reason for this is the fact that, like it or not, you have an ego that likes to be stroked a little.

Hardly anything will provide the self satisfaction that shooting an incredibly complex approach to a major airport in lousy weather will provide. Face it, not many people in the world can do that. It takes knowledge and skill and, yes, let's admit it, a certain amount of feel to be a successful instrument pilot.

As good as it feels to be running everything, it is more important that the flight comes to a successful conclusion. An unknown comic once said "it is better to die than to look bad" and I've heard that phrase used as a joke more than once during a tough approach to break the tension.

You'd be amazed to find that some people actually believe that. You'll see people continue a poor approach that almost leads to an accident just because they won't admit to themselves that it is time to go around.

You'll also see people that will get so overloaded with information and challenges that they can't tell which side is up. They will do this in an aircraft that surrounds them with the help they need but they are too proud to use it. Airline pilots rely on and use the available equipment.

Simple things like a boom mike, wing leveler, or autopilot and a knee-board can cut a pilot's work load way down when he is busy. Certain pilots won't use these aids because they think useage makes them a lesser pilot.

Pilots tell me how airline flying must be easy with all those "gadgets" to help us fly the airplane: three-axis autopilot, yaw damper and approach coupler. After a 13-hour duty day, on the fifth approach to minimums in bad weather, a good autopilot is a necessity, not a gadget.

The point is, if help is available, especially help that can enable you to look outside the aircraft more often when flying in congested airspace, use it. This help can include using passengers' eyes or using a headset to better understand ATC. Remember, an airplane is a gadget, we certainly would have a hard time flying without it, no matter the size of our ego.

TAXI GROUND FOG

Probably the hardest controlling job in existence is that of ground controller at a busy, congested airport. Traffic is much closer together, the potential for collision is greater than in the air, all aircraft are operating at the same altitude (ground level), and there is little or no radar available to monitor traffic on the ground. About the only advantage a ground controller has over an "air" controller is asking traffic to come to a complete stop.

A pilot in IFR conditions faces just as many problems and dangers as the ground controller, even more when considering the fact that you are not in the safety of the tower.

If you think it would be difficult to taxi around Chicago's O'Hare as discussed in large airport operations, imagine doing it with one-half-mile visibility in snow and fog.

Becoming disoriented while taxiing can be very hazardous to a pilot's continued flying health. More than once a collision or near-collision has occurred because a disoriented pilot accidentally wandered onto an active runway.

One of the main problems during low visibility conditions is that the control tower cab is usually well into, and sometimes above, the fog layer and the controller has absolutely no view of aircraft. They can only control the airport by referring to "position reports" from a pilot. In other words, if you tell the controller that you are on "alpha" taxiway, but you are actually about to forcibly met a DC-8 on the runway you just blundered on, you're on your own because the controller thinks you are on the taxiway.

It would be nice while taxiing around in the fog to have a good mental picture of that airport. If you operate there on a regular basis, this is no problem and you can probably taxi around blindfolded. If you're not a "local," take a few minutes before starting the engine to look over the taxi chart for that airport. Of course, you can't memorize an airport in just a moment of study, but you can get a general idea of how things are positioned.

Another taxi hazard will happen to all pilots. If you taxi directly into a bright sun, you are blind, and can stumble into all kinds of trouble if not looking out and thinking ahead.

When in doubt about where you are while taxiing, or where you are going, or even how you are supposed to get there, use the one advantage available. Stop and tell the controller you need help. Requesting assistance is not embarrassing; an NTSB hearing might be embarrassing.

While on the subject of the dangers of taxiing, when a controller clears you to a runway, does that mean you can cross all the other runways to get there?

According to the FAA, anytime a ground controller instructs "Taxi to" a runway, you are cleared to cross all runways that the taxi route intersects, except the assigned runway. If ATC wants you to hold short of anything else, they are supposed to tell you.

Because of the inherent confusion, ATC never utters the word "Cleared" when they issue taxi instructions. That is to preclude thinking "cleared" into position on the active runway. Taxi instructions to taxi say something like:

> "Cessna one two bravo, taxi to runway one four. Hold short of runway two seven at taxiway alpha."

Some airports request a readback of all runway holding instructions, most do not. It is still a good idea to get in the habit of reading the holding instructions to the controller. It is professional, backs you up, and is a very good habit. Again, if there is any doubt about crossing any runway or taxiway, stop and ask.

One last thing needed when flying a smaller aircraft IFR out of a busy airport is getting flipped by jet blast. It happens to the unwary. Give the "big- boys" a wide berth while taxiing. This might be difficult when waiting in line for takeoff, but try to allow as much room as possible. It might be a good idea to accept an intersection takeoff just to avoid jet blast. Another thing to remember is that anytime an airliner or air transport rotating beacon is on, engines are running, so look out.

TAKEOFF

Okay, it is time to "blow this taco stand "and "commit a flagrant act of aviation." Not only that, but the weather is scuzzy and the aircraft will be in the cool embrace of those clouds right after takeoff.

Plan the departure because nothing looks worse than to launch an aircraft into instrument weather conditions at a busy terminal without proper preparation. It might be fine to get a departure routing confused when leaving your uncrowded airport back home, but the controllers here don't have the spare time to hold your hand while you sort things out.

A good gauge to use before takeoff on an instrument flight is WART, which means Weather, Abnormals, Route, and Terrain.

Weather is usually what you are thinking about anyway before takeoff into the soup, but take a minute to really think about it. Ensure your ability to operate in the weather.

Not just from the standpoint of ascertaining if it will be a rough ride. Consider other things also.

If the weather is so bad during departure that it is unlikely you could make a successful return to the departure airport, select an alternate in case something goes wrong after takeoff. If you lose an engine on a twin and have to return to the airport for an emergency landing, you will have your hands full enough. If the weather is below landing minimums at the departure airport and you either don't have or can't get to a suitable alternate, you are in deep trouble.

Flying a single-engine aircraft IFR, assure enough time after breaking out of IFR conditions to attempt a successful engine-out landing.

At busy airports the situation is stickier. If leaving a major airport and the weather is below landing minimums, it is unlikely that other airports in the immediate area will have better weather because large airports usually have the latest in high-tech approaches and if the weather is really that bad, it probably covers a wide area.

Part 121 of the FARs requires airliners to file a "takeoff alternate" when the weather is bad. It might be a good idea to have at least one in mind for yourself.

Abnormals covers three things: the aircraft, the airport, the pilot. You should clearly understand the capability of the aircraft. Does all the equipment work? If not, what is left that you can use?

Anything different or abnormal about the airport? (If the VOR transmitter is out of service, it would be silly to plan to use it on the SID.)

Finally, consider any abnormalities in yourself. Are you feeling okay today? If you have a severe cold this is no time to be pitching and banking in the clouds.

Routing is vitally important when leaving a large, congested airport. More than likely you will be cleared out of the area using the SID.

Of course, the most important thing about a SID is that you actually have current procedure. SIDS change fairly often and a "Barnburner three departure" might be totally different from the "Barnburner two" in your book. If you don't have the appropriate SID, inform ATC and get alternate routing.

If cleared for a SID it is *very* important that you follow it. Sometimes routing out of a major airport is very crowded and it is very important that you stay on course or at least inform ATC if you can't.

Terrain is the final feature of WART. It won't do any good to avoid all the many pieces of traffic flying around the Salt Lake City area only to encounter the nearest mountain peak.

Examine major terrain features or problems on the instrument departure route. The fact that you are going to be in the clouds and unable to see those hills and mountains makes them doubly dangerous.

Also when thinking terrain, think density altitude. Some SIDs require a certain rate of climb and minimum altitudes for different segments; ensure that the aircraft can comply based upon field elevation and heat?

All of the above sounds complicated but becomes second nature after you work with it. Also, most of the time not every briefing item has to be done. If you have frequently flown out of Miami International, you should know the terrain and SIDs.

AREA DEPARTURE

Particulars of area departure will be covered in the next chapter, but let's review basics that are important, especially when operating IFR.

If you are flying a small and slow aircraft IFR out of a large airport, be ready for some special handling. You will use procedures slightly different from larger, turbine engine relatives for a few very good reasons. The first has to do with speed and the second has to do with altitude capability.

Look at the Atlanta Nine Departure (SID). Notice that non-turbine powered aircraft are supposed to climb to 4,000 ft. on this departure while the turbine powered versions are expected to climb to 10,000 ft.

ATC will vector general aviation aircraft away from the normal jet traffic flow as soon as possible. In a TCA the maximum speed is 250 knots as opposed to the 200-knot limit in airport traffic areas. Not only is this the maximum airspeed allowed, many times it is the *only* airspeed allowed. ATC expects acceleration to 250 knots quickly and plans the departure traffic flow on that fact.

This is an obvious problem if an aircraft climb speed is 100 knots. Because of this, you will probably be turned immediately after takeoff to a heading off the beaten path. There is nothing to be gained by following a Boeing 757 into the clouds; you would be risking a wake turbulence encounter. A separate departure path makes wake turbulence one less thing to worry about.

When departing IFR from a major airport it is a very good idea to use the climb speed that will provide the highest airspeed and still provide an adequate rate of climb.

Because you already reviewed the departure or SID, there should be minimum confusion entering the clouds and weather.

Many times at a TCA or large airport routing will make little sense, it will seem like you are going way out of your way.

The Atlanta Nine Departure.

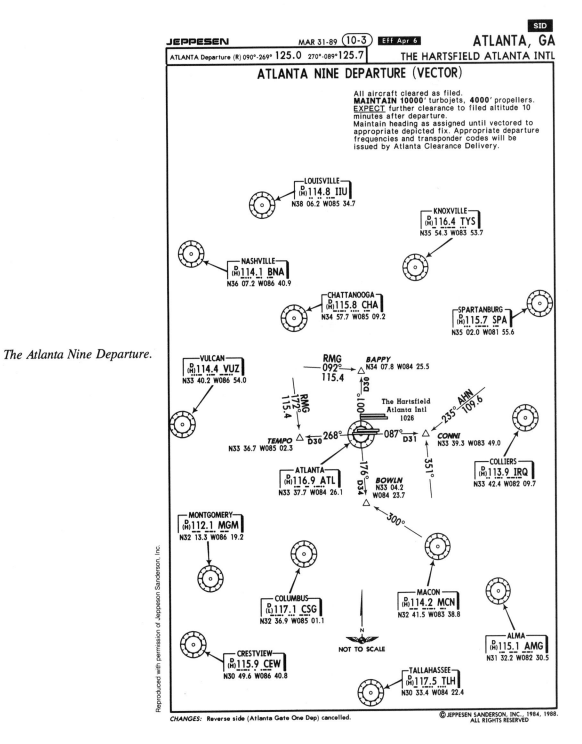

SID

JEPPESEN   MAR 31-89 (10-3) Eff Apr 6   **ATLANTA, GA**
THE HARTSFIELD ATLANTA INTL

ATLANTA Departure (R) 090°-269° **125.0** 270°-089° **125.7**

ATLANTA NINE DEPARTURE (VECTOR)

All aircraft cleared as filed.
MAINTAIN 10000' turbojets, **4000'** propellers.
<u>EXPECT</u> further clearance to filed altitude 10 minutes after departure.
Maintain heading as assigned until vectored to appropriate depicted fix. Appropriate departure frequencies and transponder codes will be issued by Atlanta Clearance Delivery.

LOUISVILLE
D(H) 114.8 IIU
N38 06.2 W085 34.7

KNOXVILLE
D(H) 116.4 TYS
N35 54.3 W083 53.7

NASHVILLE
D(H) 114.1 BNA
N36 07.2 W086 40.9

CHATTANOOGA
D(H) 115.8 CHA
N34 57.7 W085 09.2

SPARTANBURG
D(H) 115.7 SPA
N35 02.0 W081 55.6

VULCAN
D(H) 114.4 VUZ
N33 40.2 W086 54.0

RMG
092°
115.4

BAPPY
N34 07.8 W084 25.5

D30
100°

RMG
172°
115.4

The Hartsfield
Atlanta Intl
1026

235° AHN 109.6

TEMPO D30 268°
N33 36.7 W085 02.3

087° D31

CONNI
N33 39.3 W083 49.0

351°

COLLIERS
D(H) 113.9 IRQ
N33 42.4 W082 09.7

ATLANTA
D(H) 116.9 ATL
N33 37.7 W084 26.1

176°
D34

BOWLN
N33 04.2
W084 23.7

MONTGOMERY
D(H) 112.1 MGM
N32 13.3 W086 19.2

300°

COLUMBUS
D(L) 117.1 CSG
N32 36.9 W085 01.1

MACON
D(H) 114.2 MCN
N32 41.5 W083 38.8

ALMA
D(H) 115.1 AMG
N31 32.2 W082 30.5

N
NOT TO SCALE

CRESTVIEW
D(H) 115.9 CEW
N30 49.6 W086 40.8

TALLAHASSEE
D(H) 117.5 TLH
N30 33.4 W084 22.4

CHANGES: Reverse side (Atlanta Gate One Dep) cancelled.

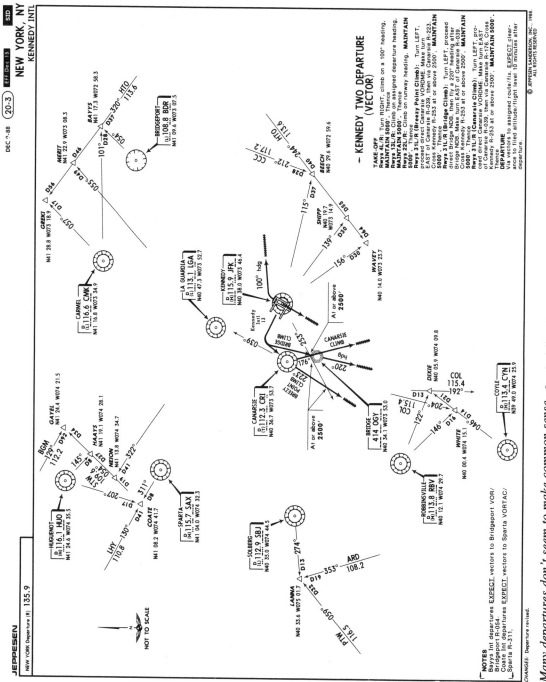

Many departures don't seem to make common sense. Reproduced with permission of Jeppesen Sanderson, Inc.

If you want to request "direct to anywhere," be my guest, just don't be too surprised if ATC refuses. They have predetermined ways of doing things in the large terminal areas and will rarely depart from habit, especially if busy.

Weather avoidance is sometimes a problem for pilots not accustomed to operating in busy areas because they lack the self-confidence to demand deviations.

If weather looks like it is going to be a problem along the route of flight that ATC has assigned, don't hesitate to get on the radio and tell you are deviating and explain. It is normally common courtesy to request deviations from a flight route, and it is also a regulation, but sometimes it is better to inform rather than to ask.

If you have to deviate from a clearance, you are required by FARs to get an amended clearance before changing course. A few problems arise with this approach. One is that if you ask for a deviation, ATC might think you really don't need it and deny it. You don't want to hear "One-three Delta unable that left deviation for another 15 miles" because you are looking straight at a huge thunderstorm.

It is almost impossible to be put in this situation, usually ATC will grant the deviation, especially if informed there is no way you can continue safely on present course.

If they don't allow the deviation, consider declaring an emergency and going around the storm anyway. Under no circumstances should you allow yourself to be pushed into flying through a severe thunderstorm because odds just aren't favorable.

When a controller denies the heading you want, but offers another that doesn't have a traffic conflict, think twice before rejecting it and going to the emergency position. The alternative the controller offers might work out okay.

In crowded airspace you do have one luxury when it comes to thunderstorms and other severe weather. You are not usually the first person through it. Someone else almost always has flown through the area and you can use their experience for a guide. In the case of the alternate deviation suggested by the harried controller, he usually will say something like:

> "One three delta, previous traffic reports only light chop and moderate rain through that area."

Even though another pilot's report is comforting and a good tool trying to figure out which way to head in bad weather, don't completely rely on them. The pilot that flew through ahead might have a high threshold of

*Although it is possible for a controller
to see weather on radar, as seen on the left,
don't always count on him
for help in thunderstorm avoidance,
especially if he is busy.*

fear, moderate or worse turbulence might not bother him. Also, weather has a bad habit of changing very quickly. It might be much, much worse for you than it was for the person five minutes ahead.

Keep in mind that ATC sincerely wants to help avoid that nasty weather. In crowded terminal areas ATC does not have the time to help. Two things are going against them; first, they have digital radar that is designed to blank out areas of weather to see traffic easier; second, their primary responsibility is to separate traffic, not be a personal weather advisor. In a pinch ATC must do their job, separating traffic. It is up to the pilot to avoid that nasty stuff.

ARRIVAL

It is obvious that descending toward and making an ILS approach at a large, crowded airport is quite different than shooting a VOR approach at a small field. The big difference is that it is *easier*.

First of all, at major terminal airports like LAX and JFK you will almost always be vectored to the final course of a precision approach. No need for much navigation to find the final approach course. Even though it is true that you will be vectored by ATC, don't lull yourself to sleep. Keep a good idea of where you are because radar might go down and you'll be on your own. Also, it is never a good idea in aviation to completely trust anyone, even yourself.

Most of the mystery of an IFR approach is taken away when flying into a big airport. Usually someone is on the approach ahead of you and you will be fairly certain about seeing the runway and being able to land because dozens have also landed.

Most major airports have a parallel approach setup. In Atlanta for instance, all four runways are east and west and aircraft make parallel approaches 24 hours a day.

Preventing traffic from flying into each other's final approach course is mostly a controller function. A separate controller might be monitoring the final approach courses to make sure incursions don't happen.

The pilot's job is to make absolutely sure which runway he is approaching and that he stays on that final course.

Let's say you are cleared for an approach, turn on final, shoot the approach, get to minimums, and see nothing: missed approach.

Two types of missed approaches at big airports are the published procedure and the procedure actually flown.

Note the missed approach for Atlanta Hartsfield Runway 9R: "Climb to 1500', then climbing RIGHT turn to 3500' outbound via ATL VOR R-180 to SCARR INT/D15.0 ATL and hold."

This missed approach procedure works well and airline pilots do it everyday in the simulator. In real life, unless you just lost all communications with ATC, it is very unlikely that you would follow the procedure as published.

In reality, after aborting the approach and making the required radio call informing ATC, you would probably be cleared straight out and vec-

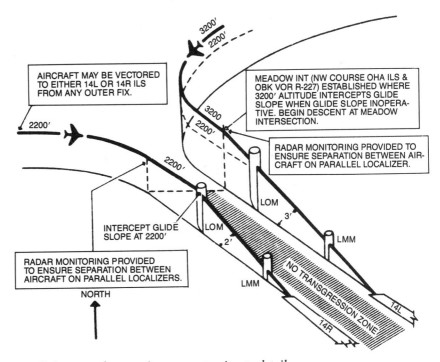

Parallel approaches require more attention to detail.

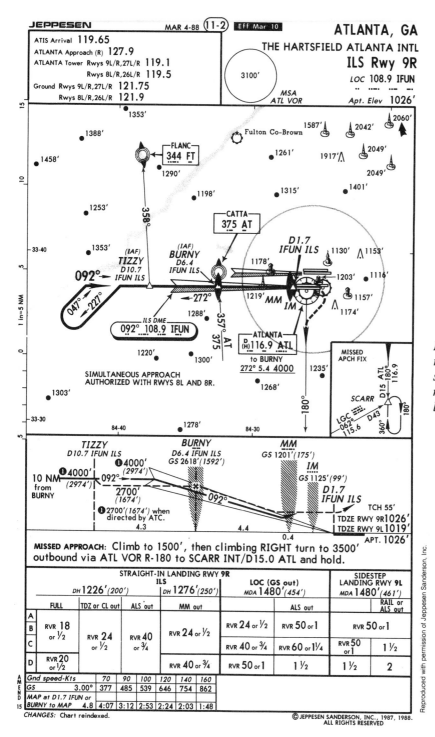

It is very unlikely in the real world that you will shoot a "published missed" at a large airport like Hartsfield.

tored for another approach or vectored to a holding fix to wait out the weather or maybe vectored to a departure route to the alternate airport.

COMMUNICATIONS LOST

Let's say for a moment that you did lose all communications with ATC during the approach and actually performed the published missed approach procedure. If the weather is bad enough to execute a missed approach and you can't communicate with ATC, don't the FARs require diversion to the alternate?

It wouldn't make much sense to hang around a holding pattern in the weather without radios in a major TCA. Also, you wouldn't have the first idea about when to leave holding or shoot another approach.

Every IFR pilot can quote chapter and verse about what the FAA expects them to do under lost communications. Almost every IFR pilot recites the regulations while forgetting two very important things:

1. If all communications capability is lost, it is very likely that all or most of the navigation capability is lost as well.
2. If you lose communications in VFR conditions, or subsequently find VFR conditions along the route, you are required to land as soon as practical. "As soon as practical" leaves the ball in your court. If flying a jet, landing on a 3,000-foot-long grass strip is not a good idea. Passing up a 5,000-foot paved airport and reentering the clouds isn't a good idea either. The regulations leave it totally up to the pilot.

9
Departure

I T IS A PRETTY DAY IN ATLANTA. THE CLOUD DECK IS A COMFORTABLE 6,000 feet with good visibility and a temperature in the mid-70s. Although it is a beautiful day to stay around town and maybe play tennis, that is not your job today. Your task is to prepare, preflight, and fly a Cessna 310 from Atlanta's Hartsfield International Airport to Knoxville's Tyson McGee Airport.

VFR OR IFR?

Let's assume, for the sake of argument, that you are qualified, current, and competent at flying the 310 on an instrument clearance and in instrument conditions.

The weather today is VFR: file IFR or VFR? In other words, which would be better at an airport the size and complexity of Hartsfield on a day like today?

The decision of whether or not to file IFR can't be made until several factors have been weighed. The first, of course, would be the weather. It would be pointless to fly out of Atlanta on a VFR flight plan and clearance if the weather en route or at the destination is below VFR minimums, or is likely to become that way in the near future. Obviously then, the first thing you have to do before making any decisions about this flight is to get a decent weather briefing.

THE WEATHER BRIEFING

There are several ways to get a weather briefing for this flight, some very traditional and some a little different.

Different forms of a weather briefing are used everyday, but not usually considered an actual "briefing." Everbody watches the TV weather people as they review the latest satellite pictures and weather charts. They even usually have an up-to-the-minute radar picture of thunderstorm activity when there is severe weather around. Even though it isn't the "official word" from the FAA or the NWS (National Weather Service) on what conditions will be, they are usually current and might be the only visual picture of the weather you can obtain.

It is a fact of life, even in large terminals that a pilot must obtain his weather briefing on the telephone, radio, or interphone. The days of talk-

At most FBOs you still get your weather briefing over the phone.

ing to an FSS briefer across a counter filled with the latest paper weather charts are pretty much over.

Many FBOs have some form of computer generated briefing that a pilot can use either for a fee or as a courtesy from the business, but the briefing is still fairly rare. Most of the time the "official briefing" from the FAA will have to be over the telephone.

When you do call, the form and quality of the briefing received will depend largely on you. The FSS (Flight Service Station) briefers are of the highest quality. They are trained to provide the best information possible and are usually experienced pilots. They want to give you valuable aid for flight planning. The only restriction they face is the pilot.

When you call or visit, you will dictate the form of briefing received. If you only ask for the Atlanta and Knoxville weather, that is probably all they will report. Although they will try to prompt you to ask for the information you will need, it really is your job to know what you need in terms of preflight information.

The FAA thinks it is best for the pilot to provide at least eight pieces of information to the briefer in order to get the best information. Take a few seconds at the onset to provide the briefer with the following information:

1. **Type of Flight Planned (VFR or IFR).** In the case of this flight you haven't made up your mind about which way would be better. In this case, tell the briefer that you are IFR qualified and you are trying to decide.

2. **Aircraft Number or Pilot's Name.** Before you begin, it is important to identify yourself as a pilot. Many people call the FSS to decide whether or not to mow the lawn. Usually the briefer will ask for an "N" number to identify you as a pilot before they conduct the briefing.

3. **Aircraft Type.** If you are flying a Gulfstream III today, the briefing will be much different than if you are flying a Cessna 172. You might want to include any special equipment you have at this point also. If you have inertial navigation or RNAV capability, it would be nice for the briefer to know.

4. **Departure Airport.** In this case, Atlanta Hartsfield International Airport. The exact airport is important because part of the briefing will be NOTAMS for that particular airport.

5. **Route of Flight.** Just provide an approximate route. Obviously the final route will be predicated partially on the weather.

6. **Destination.** In this case, Knoxville's Tyson McGee airport.

7. **Flight Altitude(s).** There is no need for the briefer to provide forecast winds aloft for Flight Level 280 if you plan to cruise at 10,000 feet.

8. **ETD and ETE.** Estimated time of departure and time en route are important for the briefer so he can give weather that means something. If you aren't leaving for five hours and just want a background briefing, it might be pointless and a waste of time to give current conditions.

Once you give the briefer this information, and remember that it should only take you a few seconds to run down all of the above, he will try to describe the "big picture." He will try to communicate a "picture" or summary of the weather conditions expected on the flight. The briefer won't read weather reports verbatim unless you request it.

STANDARD BRIEFING

If you haven't received any other information or briefings for this flight, you would probably request a "standard briefing." The briefer then has nine mandatory points to review, usually in the order below and it only takes a few minutes for them to do this.

1. **Adverse Conditions.** These items might convince you not to fly today, at least to a particular destination: hazardous weather conditions, runway closures, NAVAID outages, and the like.

2. **VFR Flight Not Recommended.** If you tell the briefer in the initial call-up that you propose to fly VFR, and in the briefer's opinion, the conditions aren't favorable for flying visually, he will inform you at this point. He is not trying to make the decision. Whether or not you press on on VFR is up to you. Just remember that if an accident occurs after a "VFR not recommended" briefing, it might not sound good at the hearing.

3. **Synopsis.** This is a brief statement describing the type, location, and movement of weather systems that might affect the flight.

4. **Current Conditions.** If within two hours of the proposed departure time, the briefer will provide current conditions, PIREPS, and other information.

5. **En Route Forecast.** The weather forecasts will be reviewed in the same order as the proposed flight: departure, climb out, en route, and descent.

6. **Destination Forecast.** The weather forecast for the destination airport from one hour before ETA to one hour after.

7. **Winds Aloft.**

8. **Notice to Airmen (NOTAM).** The briefer will review any NOTAM for the departure and arrival airport, as well as the proposed route of flight. They are also required to review NOTAMs within a 400-mile radius of their FSS.

9. **ATC Delays.** This would be any ATC delays and flow control advisories that might affect the flight. In this case of leaving Atlanta, it might be the most important part of the briefing.

That ends the required part of the FSS's briefing. You may request any other information that you feel is important to the flight.

OTHER BRIEFINGS

There are three other briefings you can obtain from an FSS that might help out.

If you have already been briefed, or just need a few pieces of information, request an "abbreviated briefing." Tell the FSS what you want, and when you received the last briefing and they can fill you in with only the information requested.

An "outlook briefing" would be requested if it was six hours or more before you plan to leave. This would be a background briefing received before going to bed the night before a proposed flight.

You can always get an "in-flight briefing" anytime over standard FSS frequencies. The FAA would prefer this on the telephone before flight. The Flight Watch frequency is preferable.

With all these briefings, the FAA probably hopes you will wait until the end to ask any questions. They will probably answer the question anyway and this will save time. If you do have any questions after the formal briefing, be sure to ask. Remember, according to the FARs, it is your responsibility to know everything pertinent to the flight.

FILE A FLIGHT PLAN

Once you've received a good weather briefing it is always a good idea to file a flight plan, even if VFR. Obviously, if IFR, you have to file to get a clearance. It would take another chapter to explain all the good reasons why you should file a VFR flight plan, here are two reasons:

1. It's free. It doesn't cost a penny to get the extra protection a VFR flight plan affords.

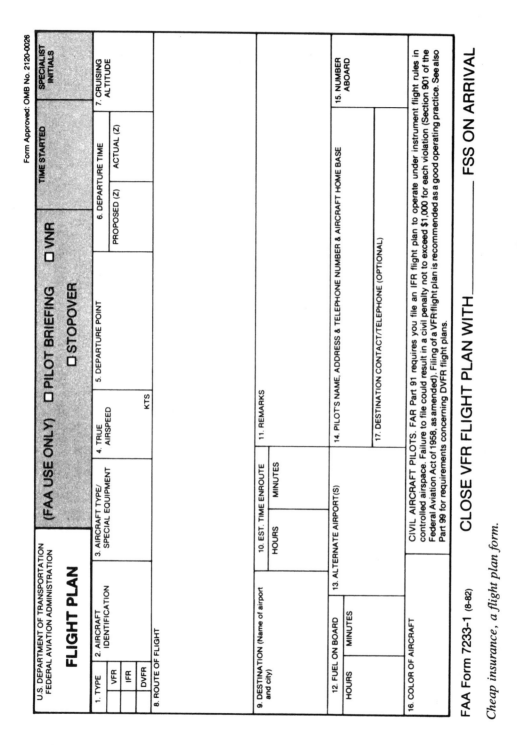

FAA Form 7233-1 (8-82)   CLOSE VFR FLIGHT PLAN WITH _____ FSS ON ARRIVAL

Cheap insurance, a flight plan form.

2. If you're flying out of a busy airport, you'll need a clearance to leave the airspace anyway. Take the extra minute after your briefing to file.

Departure control in Atlanta won't open a VFR flight plan because they're usually too busy. Just wait until you're out of their coverage, change to the FSS frequency, and open it then. Rememeber to open it on the time of departure, not the time of call-up, so it will be accurate.

OUT ON THE FLIGHT LINE

You've arrived at the airport, received the weather briefing, filed a flight plan, and now it's time to walk out to the airplane.

Before you go out, you'll probably pay the tie-down fee at the FBO. Don't be surprised to see, in addition to the usual tie-down fee, a landing fee. Most airports the size of Atlanta charge a landing fee. It usually isn't too high for general aviation pilots because it is usually based on the weight of the aircraft.

While discussing business with the FBO at large airports, it might be a good idea to include my biggest fear; keep close tabs on what kind of fuel they put in the tank.

It sounds paranoid, but the fuel sold more often at large airport FBOs is jet fuel. They not only refuel aircraft that use a single-point fueling system, but they also refuel aircraft over the wing. It is very possible that even though jet fuel nozzles on the fueling truck are larger than most general aviation fuel tank filler ports, FBOs still occasionally mix things up and put jet fuel into avgas tanks.

If this occurs and you don't catch it, you will probably get a few hundred feet into the air before engine stoppage.

You're probably in the habit of at least draining the fuel sumps on the ground when you preflight. I'm suggesting that it would be a good idea to drain the sumps into a container and actually inspect and smell the fuel. Remember that jet fuel is clear, smells different from avgas and has an oily feel.

Turbine aircraft pilots should do the same thing. It is much easier to make a mistake fueling a turboprop with avgas than the other way around because the avgas fuel nozzles are quite a bit smaller than Jet-A nozzles.

A good way to avoid this problem would be to watch the line crew fuel the aircraft, but very often this is impossible. Just keep in mind that mistakes like this can happen.

There are many extras at a big-city FBO. The first is availability of parts, service, and ground transportation. Almost every large FBO operating at a large airport, like Atlanta Hartsfield, will have the parts and personnel to handle just about any maintenance problem.

Services that are nearly impossible to find are usually available at big airports. Aircraft de-icing is the first thing that comes to mind. Catering, modern pilot lounges, and transportation to and from town are usually available at a large FBO.

You've paid the bill at the FBO, finished the flight planning, and determined that the aircraft will fly and has been serviced properly. It's time to hop in, shut the door, and fire up.

This brings up the next point of flying out of an airport like Hartsfield: start-up. Just because you are ready to go doesn't mean that ATC is ready. Usually the FSS briefing will mention whether or not to expect any delays.

Large airports experience pushes when dozens of airliners are lined up for departure. There is no use waiting in line behind all the airlines when you can wait in the pilot lounge, then taxi out, and take off. Although large airports have many pushes, it is relatively easy to fit between them, even in places like O'Hare, which seems to be a continous push.

CHECK THE ATIS BEFORE START-UP

Before you fire up, turn on the ATIS (Automatic Terminal Information Service) and listen for any possible delays to departure. ATIS is a vital part of the ATC system at practically medium-to-large airport in the United States.

ATIS is a continous broadcast of recorded information. Instead of expecting a controller to recite the weather, runway, and approach in use, and run down all pertinent NOTAMs, record it on a continous tape loop, update the information when something changes, and name every recording.

ATIS broadcasts are named after letters of the alphabet in phonetic form: D is Delta, F is Foxtrot. The following is an example of an ATIS broadcast:

"This is Atlanta Hartsfield International Information Golf. All aircraft shall read back all runway holding instructions including aircraft identification. Pilots are requested to read back their transponder code only unless company policy requires a full read back or they have a question. The 1500 weather: five hundred scattered, two thousand five hundred overcast, visibility one and one half in fog. Temperature five zero, dew point four nine. Wind three four zero at one eight, gusting to two six. Altimeter two niner niner zero. Departure runways two six left and two seven right. Runway two six right closed. All aircraft contact clearance delivery on one two one point six five prior to taxi. Gate hold procedures are in effect. Advise the controller on initial contact you have received Information Golf."

The example is pretty straightforward. Just about the only thing that you might not have heard before is the term "gate hold." This is an airline term describing a delay formerly imposed in the air.

Imagine that Delta has a flight going from Atlanta to Chicago at around 4 p.m. and bad weather has slowed O'Hare operations. In the "good old days" of airline flying (prior to the ATC strike), the Delta flight would load extra fuel, fly up to the Chicago area, and fly over a holding fix, sometimes for hours, until ATC could sort things out and put them in the line for the approach.

A gate hold allows the Delta flight to take the delay on the ground in Atlanta. The flight will still be in line for approach in Chicago, but waiting on the ground. Fuel will not be unnecessarily burned. The flight will arrive at the same time. Safety will be served by limiting the time the flight will be in the air operating in the vicinity of nasty weather.

The gate hold delay is also called a "wheels-up time." In the case of your flight, especially if going to another busy airport, the ground delay would be basically identical to the airliner's. You would be held on the ground until ATC was ready for you to enter the system.

"Flow control" is another term you'll hear. A flow control delay usually involves the en route center's air space. A center has a maximum amount of traffic it can safely handle and will limit the amount of traffic when it has to. Many times you'll run into a flow control situation when either the center has a problem, like a radar or computer being down, or if there is a weather problem, like a line of thunderstorms, in their airspace.

If you operate IFR, all of these delays might be a factor. If you leave Atlanta VFR, only local traffic congestion (pushes) would cause problems. We'll assume the weather today has not changed since the beginning of this chapter and is exactly as stated in the ATIS. The one-and-a-half-mile visibility in fog will make it necessary to get an IFR clearance to Knoxville. Remember, a special VFR clearance from a Group I TCA is not allowed.

GET THE CLEARANCE

After you get the ATIS information, the next step before engine start would be to get the ATC clearance. Most medium to large airports today have a discreet frequency for clearance delivery so it shouldn't be a surprise today in Atlanta.

You dial in 121.65 mHz on the number one comm, wait until there is a second of silence on the frequency and jump in with the following, short, and to-the-point call-up:

> "Cessna two one one five Zulu with information Golf on the general aviation ramp, IFR to Knoxville."

The clearance delivery person would reply:

> "Cessna two one one five Zulu is cleared to Knoxville, Atlanta Nine Departure as filed. Maintain four thousand, expect nine thousand one zero minutes after departure. Departure control frequency is one two five point seven. Squawk three seven one four."

This is a pretty simple clearance and the read-back would usually only be a quick recitation of the squawk. If you're uncomfortable with that, or have a question about the clearance, by all means do a full route read-back. It is better to make IFR routing mistakes on the ground.

Normally, your read-back would be a simple:

> "Three seven one four, Cessna two one one five Zulu."

If the weather was better and you decided to fly to Knoxville VFR, you would call the same person on the same frequency for a clearance out of the TCA. It would sound something like:

> "Cessna two one one five Zulu with Information Golf, VFR to Knoxville."

Your clearance would be:

> "Cessna two one one five Zulu is cleared out of the Atlanta TCA at or below three thousand feet, radar vectors. Squawk one seven four five."

Also, usually at this point the clearance delivery person would tell you to contact ground control when ready to taxi. If there was a delay they would either tell you at the end of the clearance or they would request that you contact a discreet flow control frequency for a time slot before engine start.

Let's say that today ATC said contact clearance delivery when you were ready to start to obtain a flow control release time for Knoxville. Passengers are on board, everything is ready to go, and you call them back on 121.65 mHz. It is presently around 1733 Zulu and clearance expects a wheels-up time of 1800.

In a situation where there is less than a 30-minutes delay expected, you should probably start-up and get in line for takeoff. Sometimes, if you get there early, ATC can release you five minutes sooner. At any rate, it will probably take at least 20 minutes to work your way to the front of the takeoff line. If you are approaching the end of the runway well ahead of time, ground control will probably request that you wait on a intersecting taxiway.

If you are too late arriving at the runway and miss the wheels-up time by a substantial margin, ATC will have to call Flow Control in Washington, D.C., to get you another time, so it is relatively important to be ready when they are if you want to avoid further delay.

"Atlanta ground, Cessna two one one five Zulu at the general aviation ramp to taxi."

Atlanta ground control comes back and says:

"Cessna one five Zulu taxi runway two seven right via Delta and Mike, hold short of runway two six right on Delta."

Remember that a clearance to "taxi-to" normally means you can cross active taxiways and runways unless ATC tells you to hold short. Also remember that on the ATIS ATC requested a read-back of all runway holding instructions, including aircraft identification. Because of this, the only thing you really need to read back to the controller would be:

"Cessna one five Zulu hold short runway two six right."

The controller really isn't interested about the rest; he will assume that you understood, unless you ask a question.

As you taxi out, you will almost immediately have to hold short of Runway 26R and see the reason why—Atlanta always uses two runways for arrivals and departures, if available, and as you look out the left window a Lufthansa 747 is rolling through the fog on 26R.

Ground then tells you to cross and hold short of 26L. You read it back and stop to see a Delta 767 take off from 26L.

The ground controller then tells you to cross 26L and taxi to runway 27R on taxiway Delta Mike. You notice that ATC is holding a DC-9 on taxiway Echo. As you taxi past the control tower in the middle of the field, they give a frequency change and you are handed-off to the ground controller that runs the south side of the field.

Near taxiway Mike the ground controller says:

"Cessna one five Zulu follow the second Delta 727 on Mike, contact tower 119.1. So long."

You fall in line behind the second 727 you see pass by and become approximately number 12 for takeoff.

WAKE TURBULENCE ON THE GROUND

The first place you will run into a wake turbulence problem today will be in line for takeoff. If you get too close to that 727, you can get blown over when they apply power to move up in line. If you stay too far behind, you will have everyone mad at you for wasting so much taxiway space.

Even a relatively light airliner like a 727 has to develop thousands of pounds of thrust to get moving from a dead stop on a taxiway. Usually the pilot will bring the power up quite a bit to get started, then pull it back to almost idle when rolling. Your job is to survive the first application of power.

Departure procedures from a large airport are about the same for large and small aircraft.

Knowing the correct safe distance is a matter of experience. Until you've been around long enough to know how far back is safe, play it conservatively, even if everybody else thinks you're a wimp.

Another problem with jet blast is that not only will it blow you over, it also smells. Even airliners in a long line will sometime turn their noses at angles to spare the passengers from jet fumes and spare the airliner in back. Keep in mind that you and your passengers have better things to do than snort burning jet fuel.

INTERSECTION TAKEOFFS

Many times, instead of making you wait behind a dozen jets, the ground controller will offer an intersection takeoff. He would offer a takeoff from taxiway M14 in this case.

This offer of an intersection shouldn't effect your spot in line. You'd still have to wait until the planes that were in front of you took off, but at least you wouldn't have to breath the fumes and withstand their blast while you waited.

Is an intersection takeoff safe? That's a tough question. Most airline flight operation manuals forbid it, following the old saying "never leave runway behind you." Other manuals allow an intersection takeoff in specific circumstances. Your decision should be based on a few other factors besides legality.

Obviously Runway 27R at Hartsfield is plenty long: full length is 11,889 feet, more than enough for a Cessna 310 to make a safe takeoff. An intersection takeoff would shorten it by about 2,500 feet.

Under most circumstances, something like this would be perfectly safe and would probably be a lot safer than braving that wake behind the 727 for another 15 minutes. The choice is up to you, the pilot-in-command. If you want the full length, nobody will be mad because you asked for it.

You've waited your turn and tower says the magical words:

"Cessna one five Zulu, runway two seven right taxi into position and hold, caution wake turbulence reference the JAL 747 that just departed."

You taxi onto the runway, complete the pre-takeoff checklist, set the brakes, and wait out the wake turbulence delay.

Many times in a busy airport, ATC will only give five miles behind a heavy. They will clear you for takeoff well ahead of the usual two-minute wait, assuming the heavy will be at least five miles ahead when you break ground. If you are flying a light airplane like a Cessna 310, do yourself a favor and ask for the full two minutes, unless there is some other factor like a strong crosswind that will help clear out the vortices.

After two minutes (usually to the second), the tower controller says:

> "Cessna one five Zulu cleared for takeoff, at the middle marker fly heading three three zero."

You apply takeoff power and roll down the runway. Be careful to keep the nosewheel off the centerline lights. You won't hurt them and they won't hurt you if you run over them but it makes a much smoother takeoff when you avoid them.

You leave the ground, get the gear up, and make the turn at the middle marker, tower says contact departure:

> "Cessna one five Zulu, climb and maintain six thousand fly heading two six zero degrees, cleared for takeoff."

Don't expect a turn on course until well clear of the traffic pattern. Many times the departure routing doesn't make much sense related to the direction of flight. ATC is trying to work you through departure and arrival routing, so many times their vectors seem illogical.

Eventually, departure will get you on course and hand you off to Atlanta Center.

If you were leaving Atlanta VFR, things would have been amazingly the same. You would have been expected to maintain VFR conditions at all times but ATC would have also expected you to adhere to any heading and altitude clearances.

Usually, ATC is in a pretty big hurry to get rid of VFR traffic to handle the mandatory stuff: IFR traffic. Because of this, you will probably only get a polite:

> "You are now leaving the Atlanta TCA, squawk 1200 frequency change approved, good day."

If you want VFR flight following, you will normally have to request it as ATC hands you off. ATC will bend over backwards to help, but if they are too busy with IFR traffic, don't be surprised to have them tell you that they can't help.

As always, the important thing about leaving congested air space like Atlanta's is to keep your eyes open. This is even more important to keep in mind because you will be spending much more time with your head inside the cockpit trying to maintain heading and more.

When all is said and done, the really important thing in Atlanta's Group I TCA is the same thing learned at that grass strip, keep your eyes open, fly your airplane, and try not to hurt anybody.

10
Arrival

ARRIVING AT AN AIRPORT THE SIZE AND COMPLEXITY OF ATLANTA Hartsfield International is no harder than leaving, but differences do exist.

When leaving Atlanta, as described in the last chapter, the main body of traffic congestion you had to deal with was primarily on the ground. Airborne, the congestion and traffic hassles diminished the farther you flew from Hartsfield.

The same relationship of distance from the airport and traffic congestion will continue on arrival. In this case, closer to the airport means more congestion and complications until rollout on the runway.

After landing you will, once again, be faced with mixing with dozens of aircraft taxiing about the airport.

The relationship of traffic and distance from the airport is a basic fact of life. When departing, the aircraft fly out of the airport to all points of the compass and disperse quickly, except on heavily traveled routes. As aircraft converge at an airport upon arrival, all are trying to approach and land on the available runway or runways. Aircraft cannot land nose-to-tail. ATC has to sequence all traffic at least three miles apart: five miles for heavies.

Speed compatibility also becomes a problem. When departing, ATC might offer a quick turn out of the departure pattern.

Faster aircraft would fly one departure route and slower aircraft would fly another route.

All aircraft fly the same final approach course. Trying to mix an 80-knot aircraft into a traffic pattern where most aircraft fly 170 knots can cause some obvious problems.

Preparedness is important to safety because of increased congestion faced on arrival at a large airport.

PRIOR PLANNING

Once again, there is no substitute for thorough planning before take-off. The last chapter reviewed elements of a good weather briefing from the government. Weather is not the only element of thorough planning.

VFR and IFR flight absolutely require proper charts. ATC will have very little time to hold a hand and provide finite details of navigation, excluding emergencies.

If flying into Hartsfield and the controller asks you to fly directly to Rome VOR, there is no excuse, either IFR or VFR, for not locating it and flying to it. There simply isn't time for improper planning if you operate in this environment.

This little sermon shouldn't scare you off. Although the FAA expects you to know absolutely everything about a flight, we all know that you will make mistakes and need help from time to time. We all do. Just try to head off the obvious mistakes before takeoff to a large airport.

Let's run down a personal "minimum equipment list" of items you should have to fly safely in congested airspace.

Visual flight into a Group I TCA, like Atlanta, calls for at least the following on board the aircraft:

1. Sectional chart of the area: Atlanta.
2. VFR TCA chart of showing the boundaries and altitudes: Atlanta.
3. A list of anticipated ATC frequencies.
4. A headset to hear ATC better.
5. A pad of paper, pens or pencils to write ATC instructions.

Additional material is necessary for IFR:

1. All applicable IFR charts for the area including SIDS, (Standard Instrument Departures) STARS (Standard Terminal Arrival Routes), and approach plates for the primary airport and the other

airports in the area. It would also be a good idea to carry the VFR charts mentioned previously.

2. A headset and a boom mike is always a good idea when flying IFR into a busy airport, like Atlanta. They will make communication easier to understand and will help keep eyes outside of the cockpit as much as possible, where they belong.

These lists don't sound like much, but you'd be surprised how many people wander into a TCA and expect ATC to do the navigating as well as separation from other traffic.

KNOXVILLE TO ATLANTA

It is time to "kick the tires and light the fires" and get this trip underway: Knoxville's Tyson McGee Airport to Atlanta's Hartsfield International.

For this flight let's assume that you're going to fly a Cessna 310 to Atlanta to drop off company executives so they can connect with an international flight.

A Cessna 310 pilot must be aware of airspeed when flying in airspace with airliners.

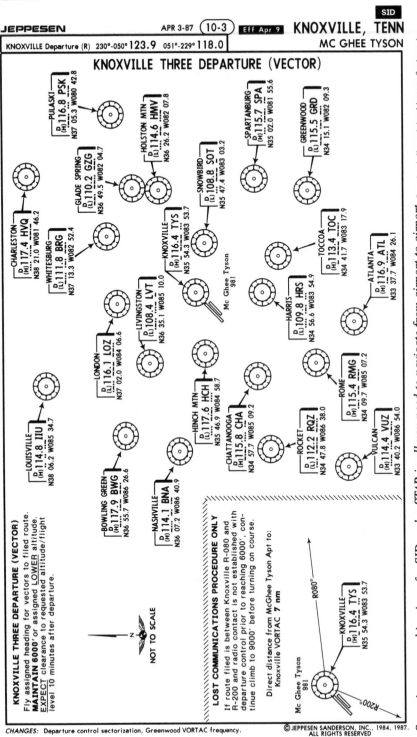

KNOXVILLE Departure (R) 230°-050° 123.9 051°-229° 118.0

KNOXVILLE THREE DEPARTURE (VECTOR)

PULASKI (D) 116.8 PSK N37 05.3 W080 42.8

HOLSTON MTN (L) 114.6 HMV N36 26.2 W082 07.8

SPARTANBURG (D) 115.7 SPA N35 02.0 W081 55.6

GREENWOOD (L) 115.5 GRD N34 15.1 W082 09.3

GLADE SPRING (D) 110.2 GZG N36 49.5 W082 04.7

SNOWBIRD (L) 108.8 SOT N35 47.4 W083 03.2

CHARLESTON (H) 117.4 HVQ N38 21.0 W081 46.2

WHITESBURG (L) 111.8 BRG N37 13.3 W082 52.4

KNOXVILLE (H) 116.4 TYS N35 54.3 W083 53.7

TOCCOA (D) 113.4 TOC N34 41.7 W083 17.9

ATLANTA (H) 116.9 ATL N33 37.7 W084 26.1

Mc Ghee Tyson 981

LIVINGSTON (D) 108.4 LVT N36 35.1 W085 10.0

HARRIS (D) 109.8 HRS N34 56.6 W083 54.9

LOUISVILLE (H) 114.8 IIU N38 06.2 W085 34.7

LONDON (D) 116.1 LOZ N37 02.0 W084 06.6

HINCH MTN (D) 117.6 HCH N35 46.9 W084 58.7

ROME (D) 115.4 RMG N34 09.7 W085 07.2

BOWLING GREEN (H) 117.9 BWG N36 55.7 W086 26.6

NASHVILLE (D) 114.1 BNA N36 07.2 W086 40.9

CHATTANOOGA (H) 115.8 CHA N34 57.7 W085 09.2

ROCKET (L) 112.2 RQZ N34 47.8 W086 38.0

VULCAN (H) 114.4 VUZ N33 40.2 W086 54.0

N

NOT TO SCALE

KNOXVILLE THREE DEPARTURE (VECTOR)

Fly assigned heading for vectors to filed route. **MAINTAIN 6000'** or assigned LOWER altitude. EXPECT clearance to requested altitude/flight level 10 minutes after departure.

LOST COMMUNICATIONS PROCEDURE ONLY

If route filed is between Knoxville R-080 and R-200 and radio contact is not established with departure control prior to reaching 6000', continue climb to 9000' before turning on course.

Direct distance from McGhee Tyson Apt to: Knoxville VORTAC **7 nm**

R080°

KNOXVILLE (D) 116.4 TYS N35 54.3 W083 53.7

Mc Ghee Tyson 981

R200°

CHANGES: Departure control sectorization, Greenwood VORTAC frequency.

Sometimes a combination of a SID and a STAR is all you need to navigate from airport to airport.

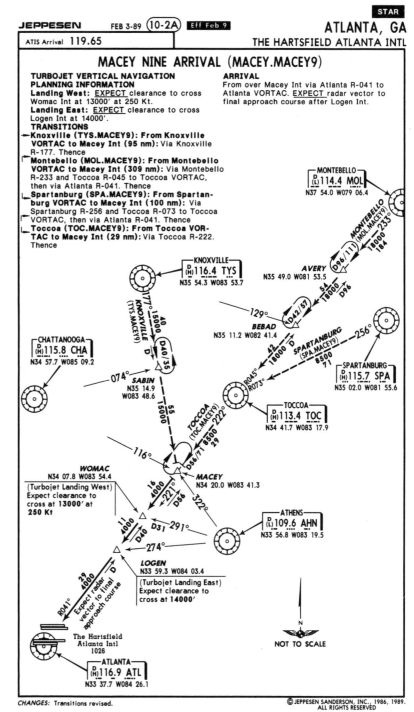

The Atlanta Macey Nine arrival. Reproduced with permission of Jeppesen Sanderson, Inc.

A major advantage that we're also going to assume, for the sake of the exercise, is that the company's president is also a pilot and will act as copilot for the leg. A copilot can scan for traffic, operate the radios, and perform other tasks that will improve the safety margin.

If you hadn't flown into Hartsfield, you would probably want to review the airport layout, its STARs, and other details about the operation.

The computer generated flight plan that you invested in, indicates that routing will be the Knoxville Three Departure, direct Harris VOR; you'll turn the corner at Harris, fly direct to Toccoa VOR and fly the Macey Nine Arrival. As you look over the arrival you can see that it is fairly simple and shouldn't pose too many problems.

If, for some reason, you were flying VFR into the Atlanta traffic pattern, routing would be approximately the same as this arrival. Instead of the arrival procedure, approach control would probably issue a series of vectors that would come pretty close to the arrival. If, for some reason, like speed incompatibility, you couldn't flow with the IFR traffic, ATC might issue different routing.

If you haven't noticed yet, a STAR is a treasure house of vital and important information. At the very top of the chart is the arrival ATIS for Atlanta of 119.65 mHz. Note that at large airports they usually have a separate departure and arrival ATIS frequency.

Be very careful when flight planning using these STAR charts. As you have probably already noticed they are set up for use by jet flyers. Note on the Macey arrival, the Knoxville transition, the number just above the course line tells you that the MEA (minimum en route altitude) for this segment is 15,000 feet, no problem for a 727, a big problem for a no-oxygen 310.

Just below the ATIS box is a narrative description of the vertical navigation to expect on the way in. Look this over because it will explain crossing restrictions. In this case, altitude will be low enough that crossing restrictions won't present a problem. A jet or turboprop pilot would have to think ahead a little more. It wouldn't do any good to be cruising at FL 210 at 300 knots over Macey Intersection if you were going to get a crossing restriction of 13,000 feet and 250 knots 16 miles down the road at Womac Intersection.

Below the vertical navigation narrative is a plan view of the arrival. This contains remaining information that you will need on arrival at Atlanta after you reach Toccoa.

You'll notice on the STAR that all the usual holding fixes on this and every other arrival is depicted. The direction of turn and location of the holding pattern are depicted. This is a bigger help than you might think. Sometimes, in situations like this, a holding clearance might come just a few miles before the fix. If arriving at 170 knots and you are given the hold five miles prior to the holding fix, you would have approximately three minutes to slow the aircraft to holding speed and make a correct entry.

Also on the plan view will be another reminder about the expected crossing restrictions for some idea of what to expect based on the direction of landing. Of course, just shortly after reaching 9,000 feet leaving Knoxville the copilot should tune in the Atlanta ATIS to get the landing numbers, therefore both pilots can start thinking about the approach and landing.

The STAR assumes a DME receiver on board and in this case the 310 has two, but each navigational fix has a crossing radial using another VOR. These other VORs and respective frequencies are shown on the plan view with the radials that create crossing radials.

Someplace on every STAR, usually near the bottom is the disclaimer: NOT TO SCALE. It is clear to just about everyone that this chart can't be drawn to scale, but it is stated clearly to make sure you know. Also, to assist orientation, there is a north arrow.

Finally, for the moment, a glance at every instrument approach plate for the destination airport. Look for notes about special procedures and hazards, like rising terrain or man-made obstructions. Later, scrutinize approaches that are mentioned in the airport's ATIS broadcast.

DEPARTURE

Knoxville is using Runway 23R for departures. After departure you are cleared to Atlanta using the Knoxville Three Departure, direct Harris, direct Toccoa then the Macy Nine arrival.

The Knoxville Three Departure is a basic vector sequence: maintain 6,000 feet after departure, then cleared to cruising altitude usually when handed over to center. The only other notable aspect of the departure is the departure control frequency, based on direction of flight, of 118.0 mHz.

It takes less than half of Runway 23R to get airborne. The airplane is relatively light because of the short distance, but you carry enough fuel to get to an IFR alternate (Nashville), plus enough for an hour-and-a-half of holding time, plus an hour in reserve.

Knoxville departure issues a series of vectors to clear you out of their traffic pattern. They then clear you up to 9,000 feet, direct Harris VOR and then hand you off to Atlanta Center. Center has the first bad news of the day:

"Cessna one one five Zulu, amendment to your clearance when you're ready to copy."

Your copilot picks up a pencil and the mike and says:

"One one five Zulu, go ahead."

Center replies:

"Cessna one one five Zulu is cleared to Macy Intersection to hold as published. Expect further clearance at 1855 Zulu. Time now 1825. Maintain nine thousand feet."

No problem, right? You have already examined the holding pattern depicted on the arrival chart and know that it is standard right-hand turns and should be an easy direct entry.

The first thing that should enter your mind in a situation like this is fuel. Contrary to popular belief, the main bandit in a holding situation isn't time, it's fuel. If you don't have the fuel, you don't have the time.

You've already planned an hour-and-a-half of holding fuel on board, plus the filed alternate is Nashville, which is relatively far away. If things go from bad to worse, you can choose a closer alternate like Chattanooga and have even more fuel and time to work with.

Usually ATC will explain why you are holding if they think of it. If they don't, go ahead and ask. If it is just a short delay due to traffic congestion the hold will be no problem. If the airport is closed you would like to plan ahead.

In this case, the hold is simply due to bad weather and traffic congestion.

ATIS reports the Atlanta weather this afternoon is poor, but not terrible: 200-foot overcast with three quarters of a mile visibility in rain; winds are 250° at 20 knots gusting to 25; temperature 60° F, dewpoint 58°; altimeter 29.97 and rising. Apparently frontal passage has occurred.

You are close to Toccoa VOR when the clearance is issued then arrive at the VOR at 9,000 feet doing about 170 knots. It is time to ask ATC a few questions.

The first request is 10-mile legs in the holding pattern. You don't want to bother with timing everything because you'll be busy enough. ATC will normally give everybody ten-mile legs as a matter of course, but if they don't, go ahead and ask, it will make life much easier.

The next thing you will need to worry about is holding airspeed. The maximum holding airspeeds won't concern you very much because you are cruising a few knots slower than the 175-knot maximum in the FARs for all propeller-driven aircraft. In this case you will be thinking about maximum endurance airspeed in order to save fuel.

Because you are still quite a few miles away from Macey, you will also want to ask ATC if you can slow down early. They usually approve this and you can save fuel, as well as burn up some of the holding time before you get to the fix.

You've slowed and entered the holding pattern at Macey with a lot of company; aircraft are stacked above you from 10,000 to 20,000 feet MSL in 1,000-foot increments. You make the mandatory report of entering holding and settle back for 20 minutes.

One by one, aircraft above that previously arrived at the fix are cleared to leave holding and proceed to Atlanta on the 041° radial at 210 knots. Two minutes of the projected hold time remain when released for arrival at Atlanta.

BEST SPEED

ATC requests "best forward airspeed for spacing into Hartsfield." This seems a little strange, considering the fact that you just spent 20 minutes of your life flying in little circles to waste time. Actually the real problem ATC faces is how to fit in your smaller and slower aircraft with the faster "big boys." They will maintain 210 knots until in the traffic pattern, where they will probably be slowed to 170. Your best forward speed is around 180 knots and you promise to maintain at least 170.

Because of the wind and weather you will be shooting an ILS approach to Runway 26R. Take a quick look at the approach plate.

It looks like a straightforward shot straight into the final approach course from where you are east of the field. Don't be surprised to get vectored through a lengthy downwind, base, and final approach traffic pattern by the approach controller as he or she tries to fit everyone into the airport.

Throughout all the vectoring it is still important to keep an idea of where you are. They can drop the ball and lose you (it happens) or you can get very confused if you don't keep up with things (which also happens). In one case, at this airport, the following happened to someone that lost their orientation.

It was a DC-9 belonging to an airline that will remain nameless, in weather much like the kind we're working with. The pilot of the DC-9

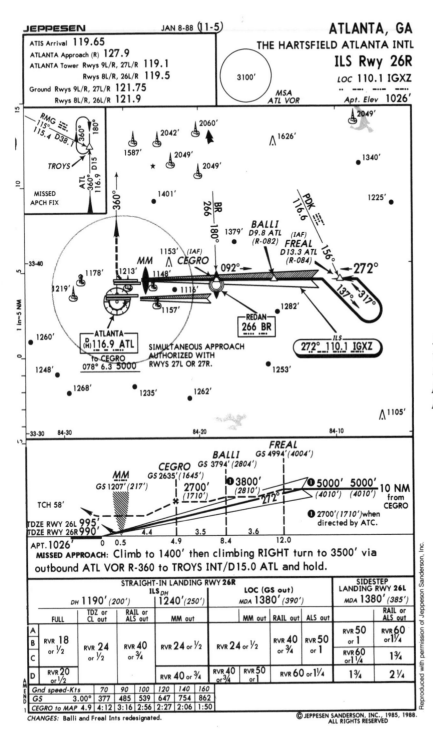

It is important in real weather to do a thorough review of the approach plate before entering the pattern.

was complaining to the tower that the glideslope wasn't working properly, there was an OFF flag in the pilot's display. The tower replied that everything appeared to be normal on the ground, then asked the pilot's altitude. Come to find out, this pilot was over the threshold of the runway on the localizer at 6,000 feet! They had everything right on the approach, except the part where they were supposed to descend.

While on the subject of things going wrong it is time to discuss operating at airports that have parallel runways and run simultaneous parallel approaches. Almost every major airport has parallel runways if the runway centerlines are at least 4,300 feet apart and meet other requirements, like having a"monitor" controller.

Don't confuse a *simultaneous* parallel approach with a simpler parallel approach. There are a few major differences. In simultaneous approaches aircraft are actually flying wing tip to wing tip on the approach to parallel runways. In parallel approaches the runways can be only 2,500 feet between centerlines, there is no requirement for radar monitoring, and advisories and the aircraft on the approach are staggered and separated by at least two miles. Hartsfield is using simultaneous ILS approaches in this scenario.

RADAR MONITOR

A monitor controller monitors approaches in progress and safety of the approach path. If you deviated off course by more than 2,000 feet laterally on the approach towards the other final approach course, the monitor controller would jump on the frequency and tell you about it. If you don't hear or don't change course back to the proper final he or she will vector the parallel traffic out of the way.

The monitor controller also has the capability of speaking to you on the tower frequency. A monitor normally discontinues the service about a mile from touchdown, but the monitor has the capability to break in on the tower frequency to give an advisory.

The controller is supposed to announce when simultaneous parallel approaches are in progress. If for some reason, like equipment failure, you are unable to handle flying a simultaneous parallel approach, you are supposed to tell ATC.

It is unlikely you would be very successful getting into an airport like Hartsfield if you refused a simultaneous parallel approach to the field. Atlanta runs simultaneous parallel operations almost 24 hours a day and would be hard-pressed to find an approach without traffic on the other side of your aircraft.

Because it is very possible that you will be issued a simultaneous parallel approach into Atlanta today, keep a few things in mind.

The first thing is to verify the arrival runway. Sometimes, even though you are coming in from the north, ATC might give you the southern runway because of traffic or other factors. Flying VFR it is still vitally important for you to verify the runway. Don't be embarrassed to ask, it might save letter writing and ATC should not mind.

Make absolutely sure you are looking at the proper approach plate, or if flying VFR, the proper runway. Especially in the clouds, it isn't that hard to tune in a localizer frequency for the other runway by mistake.

As you are coming to Logen Intersection on the Macey Nine Arrival you are handed off to the approach controller who tells you to fly a heading of 180° and to maintain 170 knots. As you do this, you brief the copilot about the approach.

This briefing will include what type of approach you are going to fly, the inbound course, and navaid frequency. Altitudes are discussed, including the glideslope intercept altitude, the decision height in both feet above sea level and above the ground, and the initial altitude following a missed approach procedure. Next, you would discuss the published missed approach and finally talk about anything unusual that might come up during the the approach. Unusual things might include unexpected weather, like wind shear, and aircraft malfunctions, like engine failure.

It sounds complicated but a good approach briefing will normally take only a few seconds. Even if you are flying an aircraft as a single pilot, some form of verbal briefing is a good way to get your stuff together for a tough approach. If you make it a habit, it will reveal forgotten elements.

LET DOWN

You are approximately 15 miles from the airport when the approach controller requests a heading of 230°, and descent to 5,000 feet.

> "Cessna two one one five Zulu, you are 10 miles from Cegro, cleared for the ILS two six right approach maintain one hundred and seventy knots until Cegro. Contact tower one one nine point five at the marker. Good day."

The autopilot does a good job of capturing the localizer. The glideslope is still above you, but the autopilot is armed to capture that, too.

Just outside the outer marker you make sure that the autopilot captures the glideslope, you slow the 310 to about 135 knots, and ask the copilot to lower the landing gear and flaps and get stabilized on an approach speed of approximately 110 knots.

You are still in the clouds, but because everybody else is completing the approach you don't foresee any problems. Should you have to "miss," it is very unlikely that you would shoot a published missed approach. You would more than likely be vectored by departure control for another attempt or vectored on your way to the alternate.

Your copilot contacts tower when over the marker and the tower controller says:

> "Cessna two one one five Zulu cleared to land on runway two six right, number two behind a DC-9 over the lights. Winds are two six zero at two one gusting to two eight."

About three hundred feet above the ground you break out of the clouds, punch the autopilot off, and land the airplane. On roll-out the tower tells you to take the next high speed taxiway if you can and hold short of Runway 26L.

The taxi to the general aviation ramp is uneventful and the passengers unload.

If the weather had been better and you were operating VFR into Hartsfield the procedure would have been similar. You would have had a little more ability to look out for other aircraft, but in terms of being "controlled," there isn't much difference between IFR and VFR at a place like this.

There, you're ready. You now have a better idea about how to operate safely in the crowded and sometimes complicated world of congested airspace.

Like any other complicated procedure or process, you can handle it if you simplify it and take it one small step at a time.

See you in the pattern!

11
Important Regulations

LISTED BELOW ARE SOME OF THE IMPORTANT APPLICABLE FARs FROM Part 91 that shall affect flying in crowded skies.

91.3 RESPONSIBILITY AND AUTHORITY OF THE PILOT IN COMMAND.

(a) The pilot in command of an aircraft is directly responsible for, and is the final authority as to, the operation of that aircraft.

(b) In an emergency requiring immediate action, the pilot in command may deviate from any rule of this subpart or of Subpart B to the extent required to meet that emergency.

(c) Each pilot in command who deviates from a rule under paragraph (b) of this section shall, upon the request of the Administrator send a written report of that deviation to the Administrator.

91.5 PREFLIGHT ACTION.

Each pilot in command shall, before beginning a flight, familiarize himself with all available information concerning that flight. This information must include:

(a) For a flight under IFR or a flight not in the vicinity of an airport, weather reports and forecasts, fuel requirements, alternatives available if the planned flight cannot be completed, and any known traffic delays of which he has been advised by ATC.

(b) For any flight, runway lengths at airports of intended use, and the following takeoff and landing distance information:

(1) For civil aircraft for which an approved airplane or rotorcraft flight manual containing takeoff and landing distance data is required, the takeoff and landing distance data contained therein; and

(2) For civil aircraft other than those specified in subparagraph (1) of this paragraph, other reliable information appropriate to the aircraft, relating to aircraft performance under expected values of airport elevation and runway slope, aircraft gross weight, and wind and temperature.

91.24 ATC TRANSPONDER AND ALTITUDE REPORTING EQUIPMENT AND USE.

(a) *All airspace: U.S. registered civil aircraft.* For operations not conducted under Parts 121, 123, 127 or 135 of this chapter, ATC transponder equipment installed within the time periods indicated below must meet the performance and environmental requirements of the following TSO's.

(1) *Through January 1, 1992:*

(i) Any class of TSO-C74b or any class of TSO-C74c as appropriate, provided that the equipment was manufactured before January 1, 1990; or

(ii) The appropriate class of TSO-C112 (Mode S).

(2) *After January 1, 1992: The appropriate class of TSO-C112 (Mode S).* For purposes of paragraph (a)(2) of this section, "installation" does not include—

(i) Temporary installation of TSO-C74b or TSO-C74c substitute equipment, as appropriate, during maintenance of the permanent equipment;

(ii) Reinstallation of equipment after temporary removal for maintenance; or

(iii) For fleet operations, installation of equipment in a fleet aircraft after removal of the equipment for maintenance from another aircraft in the same operator's fleet.

(b) *All airspace*: No person may operate an aircraft in the airspace described in paragraphs(b)(1) through (b)(5) of this section, unless that aircraft is equipped with an operating coded radar beacon transponder having either a Mode 3/A 4096 code capability, replying to Mode 3/A interrogations with the code specified by ATC, or a Mode S capability, replying to Mode 3/A interrogations with the code specified by ATC and intermode and Mode S interrogations in accordance with the applicable provisions specified in TSO-C112, and that aircraft is equipped with automatic pressure altitude reporting equipment having a Mode C capability that automatically replies to Mode C interrogations by transmitting pressure altitude information in 100-foot increments. This requirement applies—

(1) *All aircraft.* In terminal control areas and positive control areas;

(2) *Effective July 1, 1989, All aircraft.* In all airspace within 30 nautical miles of a terminal control area primary airport, from the surface upward to 10,000 feet MSL;

(3) *Effective July 1, 1989.* Notwithstanding paragraph (b)(2) of this section, any aircraft which was not originally certificated with an engine-driven electrical system or which has not subsequently been certified with such a system installed, balloon, or glider may conduct operations in the airspace within 30 nautical miles of a terminal control area primary airport provided such operations are conducted—

   (i) Outside any terminal control area and positive control area; and

   (ii) Below the altitude of the terminal control area ceiling or 10,000 feet MSL, whichever is lower; and

(4) Effective December 30, 1990. All aircraft.

   (i) In the airspace of an airport radar service area, and

   (ii) In all airspace above the ceiling and within the lateral boundries of an airport radar service area upward to 10,000 feet MSL; and

(5) All aircraft except any aircraft which was not originally certificated with an engine-driven electrical system or which has not subsequently been certified with such a system installed, balloon, or glider.

   (i) In all airspace of the 48 contiguous states and the District of Columbia:

      (a) *Through June 30, 1989.* Above 12,500 feet MSL and below the floor of a positive control area, excluding the airspace at and below 2,500 feet AGL.

(b) *Effective July 1, 1989.* At and above 10,000 MSL and below the floor of positive control area, excluding the airspace at and below 2,500 feet AGL; and

(ii) *Effective December 30, 1990.* In the airspace from the surface to 10,000 feet MSL within a 10-nautical-mile radius of any airport listed in Appendix D of this part excluding the airspace below 1,200 feet AGL outside of the airport traffic area for that airport.

(c) *Transponder-on operation.* While in the airspace as specified in paragraph (b) of this section or in all controlled airspace, each person operating an aircraft equipped with an operable ATC transponder maintained in accordance with §91.172 of this part shall operate the transponder, including Mode C equipment if installed, and shall reply on the appropriate code or as assigned by ATC.

(d) *ATC authorized deviations.* ATC may authorize deviations from paragraph (b) of this section—

(1) Immediately, to allow an aircraft with an inoperative transponder to continue to the airport of ultimate destination, including any intermediate stops, or to proceed to a place where suitable repairs can be made, or both;

(2) Immediately, for operations of aircraft with an operating transponder but without operating automatic pressure altitude reporting equipment having a Mode C capability; and

(3) On a continuing basis, or for individual flights, for operations of aircraft without a transponder, in which case the request for a deviation must be submitted to the ATC facility having jurisdiction over the airspace concerned at least one hour before the proposed operation.

91.67 RIGHT-OF-WAY-RULES; EXCEPT WATER OPERATIONS.

(a) *General.* When weather conditions permit, regardless of whether an operation is conducted under Instrument Flight Rules or Visual Flight Rules, vigilance shall be maintained by each person operating an aircraft so as to see and avoid other aircraft in compliance with this section. When a rule of this section gives another aircraft the right of way, he shall give way to that aircraft and may not pass over, under, or ahead of it, unless well clear.

(b) *In distress.* An aircraft in distress has the right of way over ll other air traffic.

(c) *Converging.* When aircraft of the same category are converging at approximately the same altitude (except head-on, or nearly so) the aircraft to the other's right has the right of way. If the aircraft are of different categories—

    (1) A balloon has the right of way over any other category of aircraft;

    (2) A glider has the right of way over an airship, airplane or rotorcraft; and

    (3) An airship has the right of way over an airplane or rotocraft.

However, an aircraft towing or refueling other aircraft has the right of way over all other engine-driven aircraft.

(d) *Approaching head-on.* When aircraft are approaching each other head-on, or nearly so, each pilot of each aircraft shall alter course to the right

(e) *Overtaking.* Each aircraft that is being overtaken has the right of way and each pilot of an overtaking aircraft shall alter course to the right to pass well clear.

(f) *Landing.* Aircraft, while on final approach to land, or while landing, have the right of way over other aircraft in flight or operating on the surface. When two or more aircraft are approaching an airport for the purpose of landing, the aircraft at the lower altitude has the right of way, but it shall not take advantage of this rule to cut in front of another which is on final approach to land, or to overtake that aircraft.

(g) *Inapplicability.* This section does not apply to the operation of an aircraft on water.

91.70 AIRCRAFT SPEED.

(a) Unless otherwise authorized by the Administrator, no person may operate an aircraft below 10,000 feet MSL at an indicated airspeed of more than 250 knots (288 m.p.h.).

(b) Unless otherwise authorized or required by ATC, no person may operate an aircraft within an airport traffic area at an indicated airspeed of more than—
    (1) In the case of a reciprocating engine aircraft, 156 knots (180 m.p.h.): or
    (2) In the case of a turbine-powered aircraft, 200 knots (230 m.p.h.).

Paragraph (b) does not apply to any operations within a Terminal Control Area. Such operations shall comply with paragraph (a) of this section.

(c) No person may operate an aircraft in the airspace underlying a terminal control area, or in a VFR corridor designated through a terminal control area, at an indicated airspeed of more than 200 knots (230 m.p.h.).

However, if the minimum safe airspeed for any particular operation is greater than the maximum speed prescribed in this section, the aircraft may be operated at that minimum speed.

91.75 COMPLIANCE WITH ATC CLEARANCES AND INSTRUCTIONS.

(a) When an ATC clearance has been obtained, no pilot in command may deviate from that clearance, except in an emergency, unless he obtains an amended clearance. However, except in positive controlled airspace, this paragraph does not prohibit him from cancelling an IFR flight plan if he is operating in VFR weather conditions. If a pilot is uncertain of the meaning of an ATC clearance, he shall immediately request clarification from ATC.

(b) Except in an emergency, no person may, in an area in which air traffic control is exercised, operate an aircraft contrary to an ATC instruction.

(c) Each pilot in command who deviates, in an emergency, from an ATC clearance or instruction shall notify ATC of that deviation as soon as possible.

(d) Each pilot in command who (though not deviating from a rule of this subpart) is given priority by ATC in an emergency, shall, if requested by ATC, submit a detailed report of that emergency within 48 hours to the chief of that ATC facility.

91.79 MINIMUM SAFE ALTITUDES; GENERAL.

Except when necessary for takeoff or landing, no person may operate an aircraft below the following altitudes:

(a) *Anywhere.* An altitude allowing, if a power unit fails, an emergency landing without undue hazard to persons or property on the surface.

(b) *Over congested areas.* Over any congested area of a city, town or settlement, or over any open air assembly of persons, an altitude of 1,000 feet above the highest obstacle within a horizontal radius of 2,000 feet of the aircraft.

(c) *Over other than congested areas.* An altitude of 500 feet above the surface, except over open water or sparsely populated areas. In that case, the aircraft may not be operated closer than 500 feet to any person, vessel, vehicle, or structure.

(d) *Helicopters.* Helicopters may be operated at less than the minimums prescribed in paragraph (b) or (c) of this section if the operation is conducted without hazard to persons or property on the surface. In addition, each person operating a helicopter shall comply with routes or altitudes specifically prescribed for helicopters by the Administrator.

91.88 AIRPORT RADAR SERVICE AREAS.

(a) *General.* For the purposes of this section, the primary airport is the airport designated in Part 71, Subpart L, for which the airport radar service area is designated. A satellite airport is any other airport within the airport radar service area.

(b) *Deviations.* An operator may deviate from any provision of this section under the provisions of an ATC authorization issued by the ATC facility having jurisdiction of the airport radar service area. ATC may authorize a deviation on a continuing basis or for an individual flight, as appropriate.

(c) *Arrivals and Overflights.* No person may operate an aircraft in an airport radar service area unless two-way radio communication is established with ATC prior to entering that area and is thereafter maintained with ATC while within that area.

(d) *Departures.* No person may operate an aircraft within an airport radar service area unless two-way radio communication is maintained with ATC while within that area, except that for aircraft departing a satellite airport, two-way radio communication is established as soon as practicable and thereafter maintained with ATC while within that area.

(e) *Traffic Patterns.* No person may take off or land an aircraft at a satellite airport within an airport radar service area except in compliance with FAA arrival and departure traffic patterns.

(f) *Equipment requirements.* Unless otherwise authorized by ATC, no person may operate an aircraft within an airport radar service area unless that aircraft is equipped with the applicable equipment specified in §91.24.

91.90 TERMINAL CONTROL AREAS.

(a) *Operating rules.* No person may operate an aircraft within a terminal control area designated in Part 71 of this chapter except in compliance with the following rules:

(1) No person may operate an aircraft within a terminal control area unless that person has received an appropriate authorization from ATC prior to operation of that aircraft in that area.

(2) Unless otherwise authorized by ATC, each person operating a large turbine engine-powered airplane to or from a primary airport shall operate at or above the designated floors while within the lateral limits of the terminal control area.

(3) Any person conducting pilot training operations at an airport within a terminal control area shall comply with any procedures established by ATC for such operations in the terminal control area.

(b) *Pilot Requirements.* (1) No person may take off or land a civil aircraft at an airport within a terminal control area or operate a civil aircraft within a terminal control area unless:

(i) The pilot-in-command holds at least a private pilot certificate; or,

(ii) The aircraft is operated by a student pilot who has met the requirements of ʃ61.95.

(2) Notwithstanding the provisions of (b)(1)(ii) of this section, at the following TCA primary airports, no person may take off or land a civil aircraft unless the pilot-in-command holds at least a private pilot certificate:

(i) Atlanta Hartsfield Airport, GA.

(ii) Boston Logan Airport, MA.

(iii) Chicago O'Hare International Airport, IL.

     (iv)   Dallas/Fort Worth International Airport, TX.

     (v)   Los Angeles International Airport, CA.

     (vi)   Miami International Airport, FL.

     (vii) Newark International Airport, NJ.

     (viii) New York Kennedy Airport, NY.

     (ix)   New York La Guardia Airport, NY.

     (x)   San Francisco International Airport, CA.

     (xi)   Washington National Airport, DC.

     (xii) Andrews Air Force Base, MD.

(c) *Communications and navigation equipment requirements.* Unless otherwise authorized by ATC, no person may operate an aircraft within a terminal control area unless that aircraft is equipped with—

    (1) An operable VOR or TACAN receiver (except for helicopter operations prior to July 1, 1989); and

    (2) An operable two-way radio capable of communications with ATC on appropriate frequencies for that terminal control area.

(d) *Transponder requirement.* No person may operate an aircraft in a terminal control area unless the aircraft is equipped with the applicable operating transponder and automatic altitude reporting equipment specified in paragraph (a) of ʃ91.24, except as provided in paragraph (d) of that section.

Glossary

Most of these definitions are based on the FAA's compilations in the FARs and in the Airman's Information Manual. Many definitions have small additions or revisions to make them easier to understand. Also, certain terms don't appear in any official glossary but, nevertheless, are used daily by pilots and controllers: slang, if you will, but still used.

(Pilots are encouraged to refer to current FARs and AIM from the FAA for up-to-date definitions and cross-reference information.)

abbreviated IFR flight plan—ATC may authorize an IFR clearance by requiring the pilot to submit only the information necessary for the purpose of air traffic control. Usually the information required is only the type of aircraft, its location and the pilot's request. The controller may request other information for separation or control. This method is also commonly used for obtaining a climb to VFR on top. It should be noted that this is not the best way to get a clearance and ATC can only grant it when their work load permits. They may, if too busy to handle you, tell you to file through flight service.

abeam—In relation to a navigational fix or physical point your aircraft is "abeam" when it is 90 degrees to your track. The term "abeam" is very general; you can be abeam a fix and still be 100 miles away.

administrator—The Federal Aviation Administrator or any person to whom he has delegated his authority in the matter concerned.

advisory frequency—The radio frequency used for airport advisory service such as unicom.

affirmative—Yes.

aircraft approach category—A grouping of aircraft based on a speed of 1.3 times the stall speed in the landing configuration at maximum gross landing weight. An aircraft shall fit in only one category. If it is necessary to maneuver at speeds in excess of the upper limit of a speed range for a category, the minimums for the next higher category should be used. Here is a rundown of the categories:

- Category A—Speed less than 91 knots.
- Category B—Speed 91 kts or more but less than 121 kts.
- Category C—Speed 121 kts or more but less than 141 kts.
- Category D—Speed 141 kts or more but less than 166 kts.
- Category E—Speed 166 kts or more.

aircraft classes—For the purposes of wake turbulence separation minima, ATC classifies aircraft as heavy, large and small as follows:

- Heavy—Aircraft capable of takeoff weights of 300,000 pounds or more whether or not they are operating at this weight during a particular phase of flight. In other words, the aircraft must only be able to be that heavy. It may not actually weigh 300,000.
- Large—Aircraft of more than 12,500 pounds maximum certificated takeoff weight, up to 300,000 pounds. Quite a range of weight. A large aircraft can be anything from a DC-3 to Boeing 757.
- Small—Aircraft of 12,500 pounds or less, maximum certificated takeoff weight.

Air Defense Identification Zone (ADIZ)—The area of airspace over land or water, extending upward from the surface, within which the ready identification, the location and the control of aircraft are required in the interest of national security.

Airman's Information Manual (AIM)—A publication containing basic flight information and ATC procedures designed primarily as a pilot's instructional manual for use in the national airspace system of the United States.

AIRMET (Airman's Meteorological Information)—In-flight weather advisories issued only to amend the area forecast concerning weather which is of operational interest to all aircraft and potentially hazardous to aircraft having limited capability because of lack of equipment, instrumentation, or pilot qualifications. AIRMETS's concern weather of less severity than that covered by SIGMETS's or Convective SIGMENTS's. AIRMET's cover moderate icing, moderate turbulence, sustained winds of thirty knots or more at the surface, widespread areas of ceilings less than 1,000 feet and/or visibility less than 3 miles and extensive mountain obscurement.

airport advisory area—The area within ten miles of an airport without a control tower or where the tower is not in operation and on which a Flight Service Station is located.

airport advisory service/AAS—A service provided by flight service stations or the military at airports not serviced by an operating control tower. This service consists of providing information to arriving and departing aircraft concerning wind direction and speed, favored runway, altimeter setting, pertinent known traffic, pertinent known field conditions, airport taxi routes and traffic patterns, and authorized instrument approach procedures. This information is advisory in nature and does not constitute an ATC clearance.

Airport Facility Directory—A publication designed primarily as a pilot's operational manual containing all airports, seaplane bases, and heliports open to the public including communications data, navigational facilities, and certain special notices and procedures. This publication is issued in seven volumes according to geographical area.

airport surface detection equipment/ASDE—Radar equipment specifically designed to detect all principal features on the surface of an airport, including aircraft and vehicular traffic, and to present the entire image on a radar indicator console in the control tower. Used to augment visual observation by tower personnel of aircraft and/or vehicular movements on runways and taxiways.

airport surveillance radar/ASR—Approach control radar used to detect and display an aircraft's position in the terminal area. ASR provides range and azimuth information but does not provide elevation data. Coverage of the ASR can extend up to 60 miles.

airport traffic area—Unless otherwise specifically designated in FAR part 93 that airspace within a horizontal radius of 5 statute miles from the geographical center of any airport at which a control tower is operating, extending up to but not including, an altitude of 3,000 feet above the elevation of an airport. Unless otherwise authorized or required by ATC, no person may operate an aircraft within an airport traffic area except for the purpose of landing at or taking off from an airport within that area. ATC authorizations may be given as individual approval of specific operations or may be contained in written agreements between airport users and the tower concerned. Note: the dimension is five *statute* miles, not nautical. It is one of the few items in aviation still predicated on statute mileage.

air route surveillance radar/ARSR—Air route traffic control center (ARTCC) radar used primarily to detect and display aircraft position.

airport traffic area—Unless otherwise specifically designated in FAR Part 93, that airspace within a horizontal radius of 5 statute miles from the geographical center of any airport at which a control tower is operating, extending from the surface up to, but not including an altitude of 3,000 feet AGL.

air traffic clearance/ATC clearance—An authorization by air traffic control, for the purpose of preventing collision between known aircraft, for an aircraft to proceed under specified traffic conditions within controlled airspace.

air traffic control command center/ARTCCC—An Air Traffic Operations Service facility consisting of four operational units.

1. Central Flow Control Function/CFCF—Responsible for coordination and approval of all major intercenter flow control restrictions on a system basis in order to obtain maximum utilization of the airspace. (see Quota Flow Control)

2. Central Altitude Reservation Function/CARF—Responsible for coordinating, planning and approving special user requirements under the Altitude Reservation (ALTRV) concept. (see Altitude Reservation)

3. Airport Reservation Office/ARO—Responsible for approving IFR flights at designated high density traffic airports (JFK, LaGuardia, O'Hare, and Washington National) during specified hours.

4. ATC Contingency Command Post—A facility which enables the FAA to manage the ATC system when significant portions of the system's capabilities have been lost or threatened.

alert notice/ALNOT—A request originated by a flight service station (FSS) or an air route traffic control center (ARTCC) for extensive communication search for overdue or missing aircraft.

altitude readout/automatic altitude report—An aircraft's altitude, transmitted via the Mode C transponder feature, that is visually displayed in 100 foot increments on a radarscope having readout capability.

altitude reservation/ALTRV—Airspace utilization under prescribed conditions normally employed for the mass movement of aircraft or other special user requirements which cannot otherwise be accomplished. ALTRVs are approved by the appropriate FAA facility.

altitude restriction—Altitudes specified by ATC to be flown until reaching a certain point or time. They are issued usually due to terrain, traffic or other airspace considerations. They are usually called CROSSING RESTRICTIONS by pilots.

approach gate—An imaginary point used within ATC as a basis for vectoring aircraft to the final approach course. The gate will be established along the final approach course one mile from the outer marker on the side away from the airport for precision approaches and one mile from the final approach fix on the side away from the airport for non-precision approaches. In either case, the gate will be no closer than five miles from the landing threshold.

area navigation/RNAV—A method of navigation that permits aircraft operation on any desired course within the coverage of station-referenced navigation signals or within the limits of a self-contained system capability. The major types of RNAV equipment are:

- VORTAC referenced or Course Line Computer (CLC) systems, which account for the greatest number of RNAV units in use. To work properly, the CLC must be within the service range of a VORTAC.
- OMEGA/VLF although two separate systems, can be considered as one operationally. A long-range navigation system based upon Very Low Frequency radio signals transmitted from a total of 17 stations worldwide.
- Inertial (INS) systems, which are totally self-contained and require no information from external references. They provide aircraft position and navigation information in response to signals resulting from inertial effects on components within the system.
- MLS Area Navigation (MLS/RNAV), Area navigation using MLS ground facilities as a reference.
- LORAN-C is a long-range radio navigation system that uses ground waves transmitted at low frequency to provide position

information at ranges of up to 600 to 1,200 nautical miles at both en route and approach altitudes.

ATC clears—Used to prefix an ATC clearance when it is relayed to an aircraft by other than an air traffic controller.

automatic altitude reporting—That function of a transponder which responds to Mode C interrogations by transmitting the aircraft's altitude in 100 foot increments.

automatic terminal information service/ATIS—A continuous broadcast of recorded noncontrol information at certain locations. This is done to relieve both the controller and the pilot of having to make repetitive transmissions of routine information.

cardinal altitudes or flight levels— "Odd" or "even" thousand-foot altitudes or flight levels; e.g., 5,000, 6,000, 7,000, FL 250, FL 260, FL 270. (See altitude, Flight levels)

ceiling—The heights above the earth's surface of the lowest layer of clouds or obscuring phenomena that is reported as "broken," "overcast," or "obscuration," and not classified as "thin" or "partial."

delay indefinite (reason if known) expect further clearance (time)— Used by ATC to inform a pilot when an accurate estimate of the delay time and the reason for the delay cannot immediately be determined; e.g., a disabled aircraft on the runway, terminal or center area saturation, weather below landing minimums, etc. (See Expect Further Clearance)

center weather advisory/CWA—An unscheduled weather advisory issued by Center Weather Service Unit meteorologists for ATC use to alert pilots of existing or anticipated adverse weather conditions within the next 2 hours. A CWA may modify or redefine SIGMET. (See AWW, SIGMET, Convective SIGMET, and AIRMET) (Refer to AIM)

charted VFR flyways—Charted VFR flyways are flight paths recommended for use to bypass areas heavily traversed by large turbine-powered aircraft. Pilot compliance with recommended flyways and associated altitudes is strictly voluntary. VFR Flyway Planning charts are published on the back of existing VFR Terminal Area Charts.

charted visual flight procedure (CVFP) approach—An approach wherein a radar-controlled aircraft on an IFR flight plan, operating in VFR conditions and having an ATC authorization, may proceed to the airport of intended landing via visual landmarks and altitudes depicted on a charted visual flight procedure.

clearance limit—The fix, point, or location to which an aircraft is cleared when issued an air traffic clearance.

clearance void if not off by (time)—Used by ATC to advise an aircraft that the departure clearance is automatically canceled if takeoff is not made prior to a specified time. The pilot must obtain a new clearance or cancel his IFR flight plan if not off by the specified time.

cleared as filed—Means the aircraft is cleared to proceed in accordance with the route of flight filed in the flight plan. This clearance does not include the altitude, SID, or SID Transition. (See Request Full Route Clearance) (Refer to AIM)

cleared for (Type of) approach—ATC authorization for an aircraft to execute a specific instrument approach procedure to an airport; e.g., "Cleared for ILS Runway Three Six Approach." (See Instrument Approach Procedure, Approach Clearance) (Refer to AIM, FAR Part 91)

cleared for approach—ATC authorization for an aircraft to execute any standard or special instrument approach procedure for that airport. Normally, an aircraft will be cleared for a specific instrument approach procedure. (See Instrument Approach Procedure, Cleared for (Type of) Approach) (Refer to AIM, FAR Part 91)

cleared for takeoff—ATC authorization for an aircraft to depart. It is predicated on known traffic and known physical airport conditions.

cleared for the option—ATC authorization for an aircraft to make a touch-and-go, low approach, missed approach, stop and go, or full stop landing at the discretion of the pilot. It is normally used in training so that an instructor can evaluate a student's performance under changing situations. (See Option Approach) (Refer to AIM)

cleared to land—ATC authorization for an aircraft to land. It is predicated on known traffic and known physical airport conditions.

climb to VFR—ATC authorization for an aircraft to climb to VFR conditions within a control zone when the only weather limitation is restricted visibility. The aircraft must remain clear of clouds while climbing to VFR. (See Special VFR) (Refer to AIM)

closed traffic—Successive operations involving takeoffs and landings or low approaches where the aircraft does not exist the traffic pattern.

clutter—In radar operations, clutter refers to the reception and visual display of radar returns caused by precipitation, chaff, terrain, numerous aircraft targets, or other phenomena. Such returns may limit or preclude ATC from providing services based on radar.(See Ground Clutter, Chaff, Precipitation, target)

codes/transponder codes—The number assigned to a particular multiple pulse reply signal transmitted by a transponder. (See Discrete Code)

conflict alert—A function of certain air traffic control automated systems designed to alert radar controllers to existing or pending situations recognized by the program parameters that require his immediate attention/action.

conflict resolution—The resolution of potential conflictions between IFR aircraft and VFR aircraft that are radar identified and in communication with ATC by ensuring that radar targets do not touch. Pertinent traffic advisories shall be issued when this procedure is applied. Note: This separation procedure will not be provided utilizing fully digitized radar systems. (See Controlled Airspace: Airport Radar Service Area/ ARSA; Outer Area)

contact approach—An approach wherein an aircraft on an IFR flight plan, having an air traffic control authorization, operating clear of clouds with at least 1 mile flight visibility and a reasonable expectation of continuing to the destination airport in those conditions, may deviate from the instrument approach procedure and proceed to the destination airport by visual reference to the surface. This approach will only be authorized when requested by the pilot and the reported ground visibility at the destination airport is at least 1 statute mile. (Refer to AIM)

controlled airspace—Airspace designated as a control zone, airport radar service area, terminal control area, transition area, control area, continental control area, and positive control area within which some or all aircraft may be subject or air traffic control. (Refer to AIM, FAR Part 71)

controlled departure time (CDT) programs—These programs are the flow control process whereby aircraft are held on the ground at the departure airport when delays are projected to occur in either the en route system or the terminal of intended landing. The purpose of these programs is to reduce congestion in the air traffic system or to limit the duration of airborne holding in the arrival center or terminal area. A CDT is a specific departure slot shown on the flight plan as an expected departure clearance time (EDCT).

control sector—An airspace area of defined horizontal and vertical dimensions for which a controller or group of controllers has air traffic control responsibility, normally within an air route traffic control center or an approach control facility. Sectors are established based on predominant traffic flows, altitude strata, and controller work load. Pilot-communications during operations within a sector are normally maintained on discrete frequencies assigned to the sector. (See Discrete Frequency)

control slash—A radar beacon slash representing the actual position of the associated aircraft. Normally, the control slash is the one closest to the interrogating radar beacon site. When ARTCC radar is operating in narrow band (digitized) mode, the control slash is converted to a target symbol.

convective sigmet/WST/convective significant meteorological information—A weather advisory concerning convective weather significant to the safety of all aircraft. Convective SIGMETs are issued for tornadoes, lines of thunderstorms, embedded thunderstorms of any intensity level, areas of thunderstorms greater than or equal to VIP level 4 with an areal coverage of $4/10$ (40%) or more, and hail $3/4$ inch or greater. (See AWW, SIGMET, CWA, AND AIRMET) (Refer to AIM)

coordinates—The intersection of lines of reference, usually expressed in degrees/minutes/seconds of latitude and longitude, used to determine position or location.

coordination fix—The fix in relation to which facilities will hand-off, transfer control of an aircraft, or coordinate flight progress data. For terminal facilities, it may also serve as a clearance for arriving aircraft.

cross (fix) at (altitude)—Used by ATC when a specific altitude restriction at a specified fix is required.

cross (fix) at or above (altitude)—Used by ATC when an altitude restriction at a specified fix is required. It does not prohibit the aircraft from crossing the fix at a higher altitude than specified; however, the higher altitude may not be one that will violate a succeeding altitude restriction or altitude assignment. (See Altitude Assignment, Altitude Restriction.) (Refer to AIM)

cross (fix) at or below (altitude)—used by ATC when a maximum crossing altitude at a specific fix is required. It does not prohibit the aircraft from crossing the fix at a lower altitude; however, it must be at or above the minimum IFR altitude. (See Minimum IFR Altitude, Altitude Restriction) (Refer to FAR Part 91)

cruise—Used in an ATC clearance to authorize a pilot to conduct flight at any altitude from the minimum IFR altitude up to and including the altitude specified in the clearance. The pilot may level off at any intermediate altitude within this block of airspace. Climb/descent within the block is to be made at the discretion of the pilot. However, once the pilot starts descent and verbally reports leaving an altitude in the block, he may not return to that altitude without additional ATC clearance.

Further, it is approval for the pilot to proceed to and make an approach at destination airport and can be used in conjunction with:

- An airport clearance limit at locations with a standard/special instrument approach procedure. The FARs require that if an instrument letdown to an airport is necessary, the pilot shall make the letdown in accordance with a standard/special instrument approach procedure for that airport, or
- An airport clearance limit at locations that are within/below/ outside controlled airspace and without a standard/special instrument approach procedure. Such a clearance is *not authorization* for the pilot to descent under IFR conditions below the applicable minimum IFR altitude nor does it imply that ATC is exercising control over aircraft in uncontrolled airspace; however, it provides a means for the aircraft to proceed to destination airport, descend, and land; in accordance with applicable FAR's governing VFR flight operations. Also, this provides search and rescue protection until such time as the IFR flight plan is closed. (See Instrument Approach Procedure)

decoder—The device used to decipher signals received from ATCRBS transponders to effect their display as select codes.(See Codes, radar)

direct—Straight line flight between two navigational aids, fixes, points, or any combination thereof. When used by pilots in describing off-airway routes, points defining direct route segments become compulsory reporting points unless the aircraft is under radar contact.

discrete code/discrete beacon code—As used in the Air Traffic Control radar Beacon System (ATCRBS), any one of the 4096 selectable Mode 3/A aircraft transponder codes except those ending in zero zero; e.g., discrete codes: 0010, 1201, 2317, 7777; non-discrete codes: 0100, 1200, 7700. Non-discrete codes are normally reserved for radar facilities that are not equipped with discrete decoding capability and for other purposes such as emergencies (7700), VFR aircraft (1200), etc. (See Radar) (Refer to AIM)

discrete frequency—A separate radio frequency for use in direct pilot-controller communications in air traffic control which reduces frequency congestion by controlling the number of aircraft operating on a particular frequency at one time. Discrete frequencies are normally designated for each control sector in en route/terminal ATC facilities. Discrete frequencies are listed in the Airport/Facility Directory and the DOD FLIP IFR En Route Supplement. (See Control Sector)

distance measuring equipment/DME—Equipment (airborne and ground) used to measure, in nautical miles, slant range distance of an aircraft from the DME navigational aid. (See TACAN, VORTAC, Microwave Landing System)

DME fix—A geographical position determined by reference to a navigational aid which provides distance and azimuth information. It is defined by a specific distance in nautical miles and radial, azimuth, or course (i.e., localizer) in degrees magnetic from that aid. (See Distance Measuring Equipment/DME, Fix Microwave Landing System)

DME separation—Spacing of aircraft in terms of distances (nautical miles) determined by reference to distance measuring equipment (DME). (See Distance Measuring Equipment)

DOD FLIP—Department of Defense Flight Information Publications used for flight planning, en route, and terminal operations. FLIP is produced by the Defense Mapping Agency for world-wide use. United States Government Flight Information Publications (en route charts and instrument approach procedure charts) are incorporated in DOD FLIP for use in the National Airspace System (NAS).

emergency locator transmitter/ELT—A radio transmitter attached to the aircraft structure which operates from its own power source on 121.5 mHz and 243.0 mHz. It aids in locating downed aircraft by radiating a downward sweeping audio tone, two to four times per second. It is designed to function without human action after an accident. (Refer to FAR, Part 91, AIM)

en route air traffic control services—Air traffic control service provided aircraft on IFR flight plans, generally by centers, when these aircraft are operating between departure and destination terminal areas. When equipment, capabilities, and controller work load permit, certain advisory/assistance services may be provided to VFR aircraft. (See NAS Stage A, Air Route Traffic Control Center) (Refer to AIM).

en route automated radar tracking system/EARTS—An automated radar and radar beacon tracking system. Its functional capabilities and design are essentially the same as the terminal ARTS IIIA system except for the EARTS capability of employing both short-range (ASR) and long-range (ARSR) radars, use of full digital radar displays, and fail-safe design. (See Automated Radar Terminal Systems/ARTS)

en route flight advisory service/Flight Watch—A service specifically designed to provide, upon pilot request, timely weather information pertinent to his type of flight, intended route of flight, and altitude. The FSS's providing this service are listed in the Airport/Facility Directory. (Refer to AIM)

en route minimum safe altitude warning/EMSAW—A function of the NAS Stage A en route computer that aids the controller by alerting him when a tracked aircraft is below or predicted by the computer to go below a predetermined minimum IFR altitude (MIA)

execute missed approach—Instructions issued to a pilot making an instrument approach which means continue inbound to the missed approach point and execute the missed approach procedure as described on the Instrument Approach Procedure Chart or as previously assigned by ATC. The pilot may climb immediately to the altitude specified in the missed approach procedure upon making a missed approach. No turns should be initiated prior to reaching the missed approach point. When conducting an ASR or PAR approach, execute the assigned missed approach procedure immediately upon receiving instructions to "execute missed approach." (Refer to AIM)

expect (altitude) at (time) or (fix)—Used under certain conditions to provide a pilot with an altitude to be used in the event of two-way communications failure. It also provides altitude information to assist the pilot in planning. (Refer to AIM)

expected departure clearance time/EDCT—The runway release time assigned to an aircraft in a controlled departure time program and shown on the flight progress strip as an EDCT.

expect further clearance (time)/EFC—The time a pilot can expect to receive clearance beyond a clearance limit.

expect further clearance via (airways, routes or fixes)—Used to inform a pilot of the routing he can expect if any part of the route beyond a short range clearance limit differs from that filed.

expedite—Used by ATC when prompt compliance is required to avoid the development of an imminent situation.

fast file—A system whereby a pilot files a flight plan via telephone that is tape recorded and then transcribed for transmission to the appropriate air traffic facility. Locations having a fast file capability are contained in the Airport/Facility Directory. (Refer to AIM)

feeder fix—The fix depicted on Instrument Approach Procedure Charts which establishes the starting point of the feeder route.

feeder route—A route depicted on instrument approach procedure charts to designate routes for aircraft to proceed from the en route structure to the initial approach fix (IAF). (See Instrument Approach Procedure)

filed—Normally used in conjunction with flight plans, meaning a flight plan has been submitted to ATC.

filed en route delay—Any of the following pre-planned delays at points/ areas along the route of flight which require special flight plan filing and handling techniques.

- Terminal Area Delay—A delay within a terminal area for touch-and-go, low approach, or other terminal area activity.
- Special Use Airspace Delay—A delay within a Military Operating Area, Restricted Area, Warning Area, or ATC Assigned Airspace.
- Aerial Refueling Delay—A delay within an Aerial Refueling Track or Anchor.

final—Commonly used to mean that an aircraft is on the final approach course or is aligned with a landing area. (See Final Approach Course, Final Approach - IFR, Traffic Pattern, Segments of an Instrument Approach Procedure).

final approach course—A published MLS course, a straight line extension of a localizer, a final approach radial/bearing, or a runway centerline all without regard to distance. (See Final Approach-IFR, Traffic Pattern)

final approach fix/FAF—The fix from which the final approach (IFR) to an airport is executed and which identifies the beginning of the final approach segment. It is designated on Government charts by the Maltese Cross symbol for non-precision approaches and the lighting bolt symbol for precision approaches and the lighting bolt symbol for precision approaches; or when ATC directs a lower-than-published Glideslope/path Intercept Altitude, it is the resultant actual point of the glideslope/path intercept. (See Final Approach Point, Glideslope/path Intercept Altitude, Segments of an Instrument Approach Procedure)

final approach-IFR—The flight path of an aircraft which is inbound to an airport on a final instrument approach course, beginning at the final approach fix or point and extending to the airport or the point where a circle-to-land maneuver or a missed approach is executed. (See Segments of an Instrument Approach Procedure, Final Approach Fix, Final Approach Course, Final Approach Point)

final approach point/FAP—The point, applicable only to a non-precision approach with no depicted FAF (such as an on-airport VOR),where the aircraft is established inbound on the final approach course from the procedure turn and where the final approach descent may be commenced. The FAP serves as the FAF and identifies the beginning of the final approach segment. (See Final Approach Fix, Segments of an Instrument Approach Procedure)

flight level—A level of constant atmospheric pressure related to a reference datum of 29.92 inches of mercury. Each is stated in three digits that represent hundreds of feet. For example, flight level 250 represents a barometric altimeter indication of 25,000 feet; flight level 255, an indication of 25, 500 feet.

flight plan—Specified information relating to the intended flight of an aircraft that is filed orally or in writing with an FSS or an ATC facility. (See Fast File, Filed) (Refer to AIM)

flight service station/FSS—Air traffic facilities which provide pilot briefing, en route communications and VFR search and rescue services, assist lost aircraft and aircraft in emergency situations, relay ATC clearances, originate Notices to Airmen, broadcast aviation weather and NAS information, receive and process IFR flight plans, and monitor NAVAID's. In addition, at selected locations, FSS's provide En route Flight Advisory Service (Flight Watch), take weather observations, issue airport advisories, and advise Customs and Immigration of transborder flights. (Refer to AIM)

flight standards district office/FSDO—An FAA field office serving an assigned geographical area and staffed with flight standards personnel who serve the aviation industry and the general public on matters relating to the certification and operation of air carrier and general aviation aircraft. Activities include general surveillance of operational safety, certification of airmen and aircraft, accident prevention, investigation, enforcement, etc.

flight watch—A shortened term for use in air-ground contacts to identify the flight service station providing En Route Flight Advisory Service; e.g., "Oakland Flight Watch." (See En Route Flight Advisory Service)

flow control—Measures designed to adjust the flow of traffic into a given airspace, along a given route, or bound for a given aerodrome (airport) so as to ensure the most effective utilization of the airspace. (See Quota Flow Control) (Refer to Airport/Facility Directory)

FSS—(See Flight Service Station)

gate hold procedures—Procedures at selected airports to hold aircraft at the gate or other ground location whenever departure delays exceed or are anticipated to exceed 15 minutes. The sequence for departure will be maintained in accordance with initial call-up unless modified by flow control restrictions. Pilots should monitor the ground control/

clearance delivery frequency for engine startup advisories or new proposed start time if the delay changes. (See Flow Control)

glideslope/glidepath intercept altitude—The minimum altitude to intercept the glideslope/path on a precision approach. The intersection of the published intercept altitude with the glideslope/path, designed on Government charts by the lighting bolt symbol, is the precision FAF; however, when ATC directs a lower altitude, the resultant lower intercept position is then the FAF. (See Final Approach Fix, Segments of an Instrument Approach Procedure)

go around—Instructions for a pilot to abandon his approach to landing. Additional instructions may follow. Unless otherwise advised by ATC, a VFR aircraft or an aircraft conducting visual approach should overfly the runway while climbing to traffic pattern altitude and enter the traffic pattern via the crosswind leg. A pilot on an IFR flight plan making an instrument approach should execute the published missed approach procedure or proceed as instructed by ATC; e.g., "Go around" (additional instructions if required). (See Low Approach, Missed Approach)

ground clutter—A pattern produced on the radarscope by ground returns which may degrade other radar returns in the affected area. The effect of ground clutter is minimized by the use of moving target indicator (MTI) circuits in the radar equipment resulting in a radar presentation which displays only targets which are in motion. (See Clutter)

ground controlled approach/GCA—A radar approach system operated from the ground by air traffic control personnel transmitting instructions to the pilot by radio. The approach may be conducted with surveillance radar (ASR) only or with both surveillance and precision approach radar (PAR). Usage of the term "GCA" by pilots is discouraged except when referring to a GCA facility. Pilots should specifically request a "PAR" approach when a precision radar approach is desired or request as "ASR" or "surveillance" approach when a non-precision radar approach is desired. (See Radar Approach)

ground delay—The amount of delay attributed to ATC, encountered prior to departure, usually associated with a CDT program.

handoff—An action taken to transfer the radar identification of an aircraft from one controller to another if the aircraft will enter the receiving controller's airspace and radio communications with the aircraft will be transferred.

high speed taxiway/exit/turnoff—A long radius taxiway designed and provided with lighting or marking to define the path of aircraft, traveling at high speed (up to 60 knots), from the runway center to a point on the center of a taxiway. Also referred to as long radius exit or turn-off taxiway. The high speed taxiway is designed to expedite aircraft turning off the runway after landing, thus reducing runway occupancy time.

hold/holding procedure—A predetermined maneuver which keeps aircraft within a specified airspace while awaiting further clearance from air traffic control. Also used during ground operations to keep aircraft within a specified area or at a specified point while awaiting further clearance from air traffic control. (See Holding Fix) (Refer to AIM)

holding fix—A specified fix identifiable to a pilot by NAVAID'S or visual reference to the ground used as a reference point in establishing and maintaining the position of an aircraft while holding. (See Fix, Hold, Visual Holding) (Refer to AIM)

hold for release—Used by ATC to delay an aircraft for traffic management reasons; i.e., weather, traffic volume, etc. Hold for release instructions (including departure delay information) are used to inform a pilot or a controller (either directly or through an authorized relay) that a departure clearance is not valid until a release time or additional instructions have been received.

ident—A request for a pilot t activate the aircraft transponder identification feature. This will help the controller to confirm an aircraft identify or to identify an aircraft. (Refer to AIM)

IFR military training route (IR)—Routes used by the Department of Defense and associated Reserve and Air Guard units for the purpose of conducting low-altitude navigation and tactical training in both IFR and VFR weather conditions below 10,000 feet MSL at airspeeds in excess of 250 knots IAS.

instrument approach procedure/IAP/instrument approach—A series of predetermined maneuvers for the orderly transfer of an aircraft under instrument flight conditions from the beginning of the initial approach to a landing or to a point from which a landing may be made visually. It is prescribed and approved for a specific airport by competent authority. (See Segments of an Instrument Approach Procedure) (Refer to FAR, Part 91, AIM)

- U.S. civil standard instrument approach procedures are approved by the FAA as prescribed under FAR, Part 97 and are available for public use.
- U.S. military standard instrument approach procedures are approved and published by the Department of Defense.

- Special instrument approach procedures are approved by the FAA for individual operators but are not published in FAR, Part 97 for public use.

instrument flight rules/IFR—Rules governing the procedures for conducting instrument flight. Also a term used by pilots and controllers to indicate type of flight plan. (See Visual Flight Rules, Instrument Meteorological Conditions, Visual Meteorological Conditions) (Refer to AIM)

instrument landing system/ILS—A precision instrument approach system which normally consists of the following electronic components and visual aids:

- Localizer. (See Localizer)
- Glideslope. (See Glideslope)
- Outer Marker. (See Outer Marker)
- Middle Marker. (See Middle Marker)
- Approach Lights (See Airport Lighting)
  (Refer to FAR Part 91, AIM)

instrument meteorological conditions/IMC—Meteorological conditions expressed in terms of visibility, distance from cloud, and ceiling less than the minima specified for visual meteorological conditions. (See Visual Meteorological Conditions, Instrument Flight Rules, Visual Flight Rules)

instrument runway—A runway equipped with electronic and visual navigation aids for which a precision or non-precision approach procedure having straight-in landing minimums has been approved.

Interrogator—The ground-based surveillance radar beacon transmitter-receiver, which normally scans in synchronism with a primary radar, transmitting discrete radio signals which repetitiously request all transponders on the mode being used to reply. The replies received are mixed with the primary radar returns and displayed on the same plan position indicator (radarscope). Also, applied to the airborne element of the TACAN/DME system. (See Transponder) (Refer to AIM)

intersection—

- A point defined by any combination of courses, radials, or bearings of two or more navigational aids.
- Used to described the point where two runways, a runway and taxiway, or two taxiways cross or meet.

jet route—A route designed to serve aircraft operations from 18,000 feet MSL up to and including flight level 450. The routes are referred to as "J" routes with numbering to identify the designated route; e.g., J105. (See Route) (Refer to FAR Part 71)

known traffic—With respect to ATC clearances, means aircraft whose altitude, position, and intentions are known to ATC.

lateral separation—The lateral spacing of aircraft at the same altitude by requiring operation on different routes or in different geographical locations. (See Separation)

localizer—The component of an ILS which provides course guidance to the runway. (See Instrument Landing System) (Refer to AIM)

localizer type directional aid/LDA—A NAVAID used for non-precision instrument approaches with utility and accuracy comparable to a localizer but which is not part of a complete ILS and is not aligned with the runway. (Refer to AIM)

local traffic—Aircraft operating in the traffic pattern or within sight of the tower, or aircraft known to be departing or arriving from flight in local practice areas, or aircraft executing practice instrument approaches at the airport. (See Traffic Pattern)

low altitude airway structure/federal airways—The network of airways serving aircraft operations up to but not including 18,000 feet MSL. (See Airway) (Refer to AIM)

low altitude alert system/LAAS—An automated function of the TPX-42 that alerts the controller when a Mode C transponder-equipped aircraft on an IFR flight plan is below a predetermined minimum safe altitude. If requested by the pilot, LAAS monitoring is also available to VFR Mode C transponder-equipped aircraft.

low approach—An approach over an airport or runway following an instrument approach or a VFR approach including the go-around maneuver where the pilot intentionally does not make contact with the runway. (Refer to AIM)

make short approach—Used by ATC to inform a pilot to alter his traffic pattern so as to make a short final approach. (See Traffic Pattern)

mandatory altitude—An altitude depicted on an instrument Approach Procedure Chart requiring the aircraft to maintain altitude at the depicted value.

marker beacon—An electronic navigation facility transmitting a 75 mHz vertical fan or boneshaped radiation pattern. Marker beacons are identified by their modulation frequency and keying code, and when received by compatible airborne equipment, indicate to the pilot, both aurally and visually, that he is passing over the facility. (See Outer Marker, Middle Marker, Inner Marker) (Refer to AIM))

mayday—The international radiotelephony distress signal. When repeated three times, it indicates imminent and grave danger and that immediate assistance is requested. (See Pan-Pan) (Refer to AIM)

metering—A method of time-regulating arrival traffic flow into a terminal area so as not to exceed a predetermined terminal acceptance rate.

metering fix—A fix along an established route from over which aircraft will be metered prior to entering terminal airspace. Normally, this fix should be established at a distance from the airport which will facilitate a profile descent 10,000 feet above airport elevation (AAE) or above.

military training routes/MTR—Airspace of defined vertical and lateral dimensions established for the conduct of military flight training at airspeeds in excess of 250 knots IAS. (See IFR (IR) and VFR (VR) Military Training Routes)

minimum IFR altitudes/MIA—Minimum altitudes for IFR operations as prescribed in FAR Part 91. These altitudes are published on aeronautical charts and prescribed in FAR Part 95 for airways and routes, and in FAR Part 97 for standard instrument approach procedures. If no applicable minimum altitude is prescribed in FAR Parts 95 or 97, the following minimum IFR altitude applies:

- In designated mountainous areas, 2,000 feet above the highest obstacle within a horizontal distance of 5 statute miles from the course to be flown; or
- Other than mountainous areas, 1,000 feet above the highest obstacle within a horizontal distance of 5 statute miles from the course to be flown; or
- As otherwise authorized by the Administrator or assigned by ATC. (See Minimum En Route IFR Altitude, Minimum Obstruction Clearance Altitude, Minimum Crossing Altitude, Minimum Safe Altitude, Minimum Vectoring Altitude) (Refer to FAR Part 91)

minimum obstruction clearance altitude/MOCA—The lowest published altitude in effect between radio fixes on VOR airways, off-airway routes, or route segments which meets obstacle clearance requirements for the entire route segment and which assures acceptable navigational signal coverage only within 25 statute (22 nautical) miles of a VOR. (Refer to FAR Part 91 and 95)

minimum vectoring altitude/MVA—The lowest MSL altitude at which an IFR aircraft will be vectored by a radar controller, except as otherwise authorized for radar approaches, departures, and missed approaches. The altitude meets IFR obstacle clearance criteria. It may be lower than the published MEA along an airway or J-route segment. It may be utilized for radar vectoring only upon the controller's determination that an adequate radar return is being received from the aircraft being controlled. Charts depicting minimum vectoring altitudes are normally available only to the controllers and not to pilots. (Refer to AIM)

missed approach—

- A maneuver conducted by a pilot when an instrument approach cannot be completed to a landing. The route of flight and altitude are shown on instrument approach procedure charts. A pilot executing a missed approach prior to the Missed Approach Point (MAP) must continue along the final approach to the MAP. The pilot may climb immediately to the altitude specified in the missed approach procedure.
- A term used by the pilot to inform ATC that he is executing the missed approach.
- At locations where ATC radar service is provided, the pilot should conform to radar vectors when provided by ATC in lieu of the published missed approach procedure. (See Missed Approach Point) (Refer to AIM)

mode—The letter or number assigned to a specific pulse spacing of radio signals transmitted or received by ground interrogator or airborne transponder components of the Air Traffic Control Radar Beacon System (ATCRBS). Mode A (military Mode 3) and Mode CV (altitude reporting) are used in air traffic control. (See Transponder, Interrogator, Radar) (Refer to AIM)

movement area—The runway, taxiways, and other areas of an airport/heliport which are utilized for taxiing/hover taxiing, air taxiing, take-off, and landing of aircraft, exclusive of loading ramps and parking areas. At those airports/heliports with a tower, specific approval for entry onto the movement area must be obtained from ATC.

NAS stage A—The en route ATC system's radar, computers and computer programs, controller plan view displays (PVDs/Radarscopes), input/output devices, and the related communications equipment which are integrated to form the heart of the automated IFR air traffic control system. This equipment performs Flight Data Processing (FDP) and Radar Data Processing (RDP). It interfaces with automated terminal systems and is used in the control of en route IFR aircraft. (Refer to AIM)

National Airspace System/NAS—The common network of U.S. airspace; air navigation facilities, equipment and services, airports or landing areas; aeronautical charts, information and services; rules, regulations and procedures, technical information, and manpower and material. Included are system components shared jointly with the military.

national beacon code allocation plan airspace/NBCAP airspace—Airspace over United States territory located within the North American continent between Canada and Mexico, including adjacent territorial waters outward to about boundaries of oceanic control areas (CTA)/Flight Information regions (FIR). (See Flight Information Region)

National Flight Data Center/NFDC—A facility in Washington D.C., established by FAA to operate a central aeronautical information service for the collection, validation, and dissemination of aeronautical data in support of the activities of government, industry, and the aviation community. The information is published in the National Flight Data Digest. (See National Flight Data Digest)

NAVAID classes—VOR VORTAC, and TACAN aids are classed according to their operational use. The three classes of NAVAID's are:

> T—Terminal
> L-Low altitude
> H—High altitude

The normal service range for T,L, and H class aids is found in the AIM. Certain operational requirements make it necessary to use some of these aids at greater service ranges than specified. Extended range is made possible through flight inspection determinations. Some aids also have lesser service range due to location, terrain, frequency protection, etc. Restrictions to service range are listed in Airport/Facility Directory.

negative contact—Used by pilots to inform ATC that:

- Previously issued traffic is not in sight. It may be followed by the pilot's request for the controller to provide assistance in avoiding the traffic.
- They were unable to contact ATC on a particular frequency.

nonapproach control tower—Authorizes aircraft to land or takeoff at the airport controlled by the tower or to transit the airport traffic area. The primary function of a nonapproach control tower is the sequencing of aircraft in the traffic pattern and on the landing area. Nonapproach control towers also separate aircraft operating under instrument flight rules clearances from approach controls and centers. They provide ground control services to aircraft, vehicles, personnel, and equipment on the airport movement area.

numerous targets vicinity (location)—A traffic advisory issued by ATC to advise pilots that targets on the radarscope are too numerous to issue individually. (See Traffic Advisories)

option approach—An approach requested and conducted by a pilot which will result in either a touch-and-go, missed approach, low approach, stop-and-go, or full stop landing. (See Cleared for the Option) (Refer to AIM)

outer area (associated with ARSA)—Nonregulatory airspace surrounding designated ARSA airports wherein ATC provides radar vectoring and sequencing on a full-time basis for all IFR and participating VFR aircraft. The service provided in the outer area is called ARSA service which includes: IFR/IFR-standard IFR separation; IFR/VFR-traffic advisories and conflict resolution; and VFR/VFR-traffic advisories and, as appropriate, safety alerts. The normal radius will be 20 nautical miles with some variations based on site-specific requirements. The outer area extends outward from the primary ARSA airport and extends from the lower limits of radar/radio coverage up to the ceiling of the approach control's delegated airspace excluding the ARSA and other airspace as appropriate. (See Controlled Airspace-Airport Radar Service Area/ARSA, Conflict resolution)

overhead approach/360 overhead—A series of predetermined maneuvers prescribed for VFR arrival of military aircraft (often in formation) for entry into the VFR traffic pattern and to proceed to a landing. The pattern usually specifies the following:

- The radio contact required of the pilot.
- The speed to be maintained.
- An initial approach 3 to 5 miles in length.
- An elliptical pattern consisting of two 180 degree turns.
- A break point at which the first 180 degree turn is started.
- The direction of turns.
- Altitude (at least 500 feet above the conventional pattern).

- A "rollout" on final approach not less than 1/4 mile from the landing threshold and not less than 300 feet above the ground.

pan-pan—The international radio-telephony urgency signal. When repeated three times, indicates uncertainty or alert followed by the nature of the urgency. (See MAYDAY) (Refer to AIM)

parallel ILS/MLS approaches—Approaches to parallel runways by IFR aircraft which, when established inbound toward the airport on the adjacent final approach courses, are radar-separated by at least 2 miles. (See Final Approach Course, Simultaneous ILS/MLS Approaches).

pilot briefing/preflight pilot briefing—A service provided by the FSS to assist pilots in flight planning. Briefing items may include weather information, NOTAMS, military activities, flow control information, and other items as requested. (Refer to AIM)

pilot automatic telephone weather answering service/PATWAS—A continuous telephone recording containing current and forecast weather information for pilots. (See Flight Service Station) (Refer to AIM)

pilot's discretion—When used in conjunction with altitude assignments, means that ATC has offered the pilot the option of starting climb or descent whenever he wishes and conducting the climb or descent at any rate he wishes. He may temporarily level off at any intermediate altitude. However, once he has vacated an altitude, he may not return to that altitude.

positive control—The separation of all air traffic within designated airspace by air traffic control. (See Positive Control Area)

preferential routes—Preferential routes (PDR's, PAR's, and PDAR's) are adapted in ARTCC computers to accomplish inter/intrafacility controller coordination and to assure that flight data is posted at the proper control positions. Locations having a need for these specific inbound and outbound routes normally publish such routes in local facility bulletins, and their use by pilots minimizes flight plan route amendments. When the work load or traffic situation permits, controllers normally provide radar vectors or assign requested routes to minimize circuitous routing. Preferential routes are usually confined to one ARTCC's area and are referred to by the following names or acronyms:

- Preferential Departure Route/PDR—A specific departure route from an airport or terminal area to an en route point where there is no further need for flow control. It may be included in a

Standard Instrument Departure (SID) or a Preferred IFR route.

- Preferential Arrival Route/PAR—A specific arrival route from an appropriate en route point to an airport or terminal area. It may be included in a Standard Terminal Arrival (STAR) or Preferred IFR Route. The abbreviation "PAR" is used primarily within the ARTCC and should not be confused with the abbreviation for Precision Approach Radar.
- Preferential Departure and Arrival Route/PDAR—A route between two terminals which are within or immediately adjacent to one ARTCC's area. PDAR's are not synonymous with Preferred IFR Routes but may be listed as such as they do accomplish essentially the same purpose. (See Preferred IFR Routes, NAS Stage A)

preferred IFR routes—Routes established between busier airports to increase system efficiency and capacity. They normally extend through one or more ARTCC areas and are designed to achieve balanced traffic flows among high density terminals. IFR clearances are issued on the basis of these routes except when severe weather avoidance procedures or other factors dictate otherwise. Preferred IFR Routes are listed in the Airport/Facility Directory. If a flight is planned to or from an area having such routes but the departure or arrival point is not listed in the Airport/Facility Directory, pilots may use that part of a Preferred IFR Route which is appropriate for the departure or arrival point that is listed. Preferred IFR Routes are correlated with SID's and STAR'S and may be defined by airways, jet routes, direct routes between NAVAID's, Waypoints, NAVAID radials/DME, or any combinations thereof. (See Standard Instrument Departure, Standard Terminal Arrival, Preferential Routes, Center's Area) (Refer to Airport/Facility Directory and Notices to Airmen Publication)

profile descent—An uninterrupted descent (except where level flight is required for speed adjustment; e.g., 250 knots at 10,000 feet MSL) from cruising altitude/level to interception of a glide slope or to minimum altitude specified for the initial or intermediate approach segment of a non-precision instrument approach. The profile descent normally terminates at the approach gate or where the glide slope or other appropriate minimum altitude is intercepted.

published route—A route for which an IFR altitude has been established and published; e.g., Federal Airways, Jet Routes, Area Navigation Routes, Specified Direct Routes.

quick look A feature of NAS Stage A and ARTS which provides the controller the capability to display full data blocks of tracked aircraft from other control positions.

quota flow control/QFLOW—A flow control procedure by which the Central Flow Control Function (CFCF) restricts traffic to the ARTC Center area having an impacted airport, thereby avoiding sector/area saturation. (See Air Traffic Control Systems Command Center) (Refer to Airport/Facility Directory)

radar/radio detection and ranging—A device which, by measuring the time interval between transmission and reception of radio pulses and correlating the angular orientation of the radiated antenna beam or beams in azimuth and/or elevation, provides information on range, azimuth, and/or elevation of objects in the path of the transmitted pulses.

radar approach control facility—A terminal ATC facility that uses radar and nonradar capabilities to provide approach control services to aircraft arriving, departing, or transiting airspace controlled by the facility (See Approach Control Service). Provides radar ATC services to aircraft operating in the vicinity of one or more civil and/or military airports in a terminal area. The facility may provide services of a ground controlled approach (GCA); i.e., ASR and PAR approaches. A radar approach control facility may be operated by FAA, USAF, US Army, USN, USMC, or jointly by FAA and a military service. Specific facility nomenclatures are used for administrative purposes only and are related to the physical location of the facility and the operating service generally as follows:

- Army Radar Approach Control/ARAC (Army)
- Radar Air Traffic Control Facility/RATCF (Navy/FAA)
- Terminal Radar Approach Control/TRACON (FAA).
- Tower/Airport Traffic Control Tower/ATCT (FAA). (Only those towers delegated approach control authority.)

radar contact

- Used by ATC to inform an aircraft that it is identified on the radar display and radar flight following will be provided until radar identification is terminated. Radar service may also be provided within the limits of necessity and capability. When a pilot is informed of "radar contact," he automatically discontinues reporting over compulsory reporting points. (See Radar

Flight Following, Radar Contact Lost, Radar Service, Radar Service Terminated). (Refer to AIM)
- The term used to inform the controller that the aircraft is identified and approval is granted for the aircraft to enter the receiving controllers airspace.

radar contact lost—Used by ATC to inform a pilot that radar identification of his aircraft has been lost. The loss may be attributed to several things including the aircraft's merging with weather or ground clutter, the aircraft's flying below radar line of sight, the aircraft's entering an area of poor radar return, or a failure of the aircraft transponder or the ground radar equipment. (See Clutter, Radar Contact)

radar flight following—The observation of the progress of radar identified aircraft, whose primary navigation is being provided by the pilot, wherein the controller retains and correlates the aircraft identity with the appropriate target or target symbol displayed on the radarscope. (See Radar Contact, Radar Service) (Refer to AIM)

radar service terminated—Used by ATC to inform a pilot that he will no longer be provided any of the services that could be received while in radar contact. Radar service is automatically terminated, and the pilot is not advised in the following cases:

- An aircraft cancels its IFR flight plan, except within a TCA, TRSA, ARSA, or where Stage II service is provided.
- An aircraft conducting an instrument, visual, or contact approach has landed or has been instructed to change to advisory frequency.
- An arriving VFR aircraft, receiving radar service to a tower-controlled airport within a TCA, TRSA, ARSA, or where Stage II service is provided, has landed; or to all other airports, is instructed to change to tower or advisory frequency.
- An aircraft completes a radar approach.

radar traffic advisories—Advisories issued to alert pilots to known or observed radar traffic which may affect the intended route of flight of their aircraft. (See Traffic Advisories)

radial—A magnetic bearing extending from a VOR/VORTAC/TACAN navigation facility.

receiving controller/facility—A controller/facility receiving control of an aircraft from another controller/facility.

release time—A departure time restriction issued to a pilot by ATC (either directly or through an authorized relay) when necessary to separate a departing aircraft from other traffic.

request full route clearance/FRC—Used by pilots to request that the entire route of flight be read verbatim in an ATC clearance. Such request should be made to preclude receiving an ATC clearance based on the original filed flight plan when a filed IFR flight plan has been revised by the pilot, company, or operations prior to departure.

resume own navigation—Used by ATC to advise a pilot to resume his own navigational responsibility. It is issued after completion of a radar vector or when radar contact is lost while the aircraft is being radar vectored. (See Radar Contact Lost, Radar Service Terminated)

roger—I have received all of your last transmission. It should not be used to answer a question requiring a yes or a no answer. (See Affirmative, Negative)

runway heading—The magnetic direction indicated by the runway number. When cleared to "fly/maintain runway heading," pilots are expected to comply with the ATC clearance by flying the heading indicated by the runway number without applying any drift correction; e.g., Runway 4, 040° magnetic heading; Runway 20, 200° magnetic heading.

runway profile descent—An instrument flight rules (IFR) air traffic control arrival procedure to a runway published for pilot use in graphic and/or textual form and may be associated with a STAR. Runway Profile Descents provide routing and may depict crossing altitudes, speed restrictions, and headings to be flown from the en route structure to the point where the pilot will receive clearance for the execute an instrument approach procedure. A Runway Profile Descent may apply to more than one runway if so stated on the chart. (Refer to AIM)

runway use program—A noise abatement runway selection plan designed to enhance noise abatement efforts with regard to airport communities for arriving and departing aircraft. These plans are developed into runway use programs and apply to all turbojet aircraft 12,500 pounds or heavier; turbojet aircraft less than 12,500 pounds are included only if the airport proprietor determines that the aircraft creates a noise problem. Runway use programs are coordinated with FAA offices, and safety criteria used in these programs are developed by the

Office of Flight Operations. Runway use programs are administered by the Air Traffic Service as "Formal" or "Informal" programs.

- Formal Runway Use Program—An approved noise abatement program which is defined and acknowledged in a Letter of Understanding between Flight Operations, Air Traffic Service, the airport proprietor, and the users. Once established, participation in the program is mandatory for aircraft operators and pilots as provided for in FAR 91.87.
- Informal Runway Use Program—An approved noise abatement program which does not require a Letter of Understanding, and participation in the program is voluntary for aircraft operators/ pilots.

safety alert—A safety alert issued by ATC to aircraft under their control if ATC is aware the aircraft is at an altitude which, in the controller's judgement, places the aircraft in unsafe proximity to terrain, obstructions, or other aircraft. The controller may discontinue the issuance of further alerts if the pilot advises he is taking action to correct the situation or has the other aircraft in sight.

- Terrain/Obstruction Alert—A safety alert issued by ATC to aircraft under their control if ATC is aware the aircraft is at an altitude which, in the controller's judgement, places the aircraft in unsafe proximity to terrain/obstructions; e.g., "Low Altitude Alert, check your altitude immediately."
- Aircraft Conflict Alert—A safety alert issued by ATC to aircraft under their control if ATC is aware of an aircraft that is not under their control at an altitude which, in the controller's judgement, places both aircraft in unsafe proximity to each other. With the alert, ATC will offer the pilot an alternate course of action when feasible; e.g., "Traffic Alert, advise you turn right heading zero niner zero or climb to eight thousand immediately."

The issuance of safety alert is contingent upon the capability of the controller to have an awareness of an unsafe condition. The course of action provided will be predicated on other traffic under ATC control. Once the alert is issued, it is solely the pilot's prerogative to determine what course of action, if any, he will take.

say again—Used to request a repeat of the last transmission. Usually specifies transmission or portion thereof not understood or received; e.g., "Say again all after ABRAMVOR."

say altitude—Used by ATC to ascertain an aircraft's specific altitude/flight level. When the aircraft is climbing or descending, the pilot should state the indicated altitude rounded to the nearest 100 feet.

say heading—Used by ATC to request an aircraft heading. The pilot should state the actual heading of the aircraft.

see and avoid—A visual procedure wherein pilots of aircraft flying in visual meteorological conditions (VMC), regardless of type of flight plan, are charged with the responsibility to observe the presence of other aircraft and to maneuver their aircraft as required to avoid the other aircraft. Right-of-way rules are contained in FAR, Part 91. (See Instrument Flight Rules, Visual Flight Rules, Visual Meteorological Conditions, Instrument Meteorological Conditions)

severe weather avoidance plan/SWAP—An approved plan to minimize the effect of severe weather on traffic flows in impacted terminal and/or ARTCC areas. SWAP is normally implemented to provide the least disruption to the ATC system when flight through portions of airspace is difficult or impossible due to severe weather.

severe weather forecast alerts/AWW—Preliminary messages issued in order to alert users that a Severe Weather Watch Bulletin (WW) is being issued. These messages define areas of possible severe thunderstorms or tornado activity. The messages are unscheduled and issued as required by the National Severe Storm Forecast Center at Kansas City, Missouri. (See SIGMET, Convective SIGMET, CWA, and AIRMET)

short range clearance—A clearance issued to a departing IFR flight which authorizes IFR flight to a specific fix short of the destination while air traffic control facilities are coordinating and obtaining the complete clearance.

sidestep maneuver—A visual maneuver accomplished by a pilot at the completion of an instrument approach to permit a straight-in landing on a parallel runway not more than 1,200 feet to either side of the runway to which the instrument approach was conducted. (Refer to AIM)

simultaneous ILS/MLS approaches—An approach system permitting simultaneous ILS/MLS approaches to airports having parallel runways separated by at least 4,300 feet between centerlines. Integral parts of a total system are ILS/MLS, radar, communications, ATC procedure, and appropriate airborne equipment. (See Parallel Runways) (Refer to AIM)

special emergency—A condition of air piracy or other hostile act by a person(s) aboard an aircraft which threatens the safety of the aircraft or its passengers.

special use airspace—Airspace of defined dimensions identified by an area on the surface of the earth wherein activities must be confined because of their nature and/or wherein limitations may be imposed upon aircraft operations that are not a part of those activities. Types of special use airspaces are:

- Alert Area—Airspace which may contain a high volume of pilot training activities or an unusual type of aerial activity, neither of which is hazardous to aircraft. Alert Areas are depicted on aeronautical charts for the information of nonparticipating pilots. All activities within an Alert Area are conducted in accordance with Federal Aviation regulations, and pilots of participating aircraft as well as pilots transiting the area are equally responsible for collision avoidance.
- Controlled Firing Area—Airspace wherein activities are conducted under conditions so controlled as to eliminate hazards to nonparticipating aircraft and to ensure the safety of persons and property on the ground.
- Military Operations Area (MOA)—An MOA is an airspace assignment of defined vertical and lateral dimensions established outside positive control areas to separate/segregate certain military activities from IFR traffic and to identify for VFR traffic where these activities are conducted. (Refer to AIM)
- Prohibited Area—Designed airspace within which the flight of aircraft is prohibited. (Refer to En Route Charts, AIM).
- Restricted Area—Airspace designated under FAR, Part 73, within which the flight of aircraft, while not wholly prohibited, is subject to restriction. Most restricted areas are designated joint use and IFR/VFR operations in the area may be authorized by the controlling ATC facility when it is not being utilized by the using agency. Restricted areas are depicted on en route charts. Where joint use is authorized, the name of the ATC controlling facility is also shown. (Refer to FAR, Part 73 and AIM)
- Warning Area—Airspace which may contain hazards to nonparticipating aircraft in international airspace.

special VFR conditions—Weather conditions in a control zone which are less than basic VFR and in which some aircraft are permitted flight under Visual Flight Rules. (See Special VFR Operations) (Refer to FAR, Part 91)

special VFR operations—Aircraft operating in accordance with clearances within control zones in weather conditions less than the basic VFR weather minima. Such operations must be requested by the pilot and approved by ATC. (See Special VFR Conditions)

speed adjustment—An ATC procedure used to request pilots to adjust aircraft speed to a specific value for the purpose of providing desired spacing. Pilots are expected to maintain a speed of plus or minus 10 knots or 0.02 mach number of the specified speed. Examples of speed adjustments are:

- "Increase/reduce speed to mach point (number)."
- "Increase/reduce speed to (speed in knots)" or "Increase/reduce speed (number of knots) knots."

squawk—Activate specific modes/codes/functions on the aircraft transponder; e.g., "Squawk three/alpha, two one zero five, low." (See Transponder)

standard instrument departure/SID—A preplanned instrument flight rule (IFR) air traffic control departure procedure printed for pilot use in graphic and/or textual form. SID's provide transition from the terminal to the appropriate en route structure. (See IFR Takeoff Minima and Departure Procedures) (Refer to AIM)

standard terminal arrival/STAR—A preplanned instrument flight rule (IFR) air traffic control arrival procedure published for pilot use in graphic and/or textual form. STAR's provide transition from the en route structure to an outer fix or an instrument approach fix/arrival way point in the terminal area.

stepdown fix—A fix permitting additional descent within a segment of an instrument approach procedure by identifying a point at which a controlling obstacle has been safely over-flown.

stop altitude squawk—Used by ATC to inform an aircraft to turn off the automatic altitude reporting feature of its transponder. It is issued when the verbally reported altitude varies 300 feet or more from the automatic altitude report. (See Altitude Readout, Transponder)

stop and go—A procedure wherein an aircraft will land, make a complete stop on the runway, and then commence a takeoff from that point. (See Low Approach, Option Approach)

stopover flight plan—A flight plan format which permits in a single submission the filing of a sequence of flight plans through interim full-stop destinations to a final destination.

stop squawk—Used by ATC to tell the pilot to turn specified functions of the aircraft transponder off. (See Stop Altitude Squawk, Transponder)

straight-in approach-IFR—An instrument approach wherein final approach is begun without first having executed a procedure turn, not necessarily completed with a straight-in landing or made to straight-in landing minimums. (See Straight-in Landing, Landing Minimums, Straight-In Approach-VFR)

straight-in approach—VFR—Entry into the traffic pattern by interception of the extended runway centerline (final approach course) without executing any other portion of the traffic pattern. (See Traffic Pattern)

straight-in landing—A landing made on a runway aligned within 30° of the final approach course following completion of an instrument approach.

surveillance approach—An instrument approach wherein the air traffic controller issues instructions, for pilot compliance, based on aircraft position in relation to the final approach course (azimuth), and the distance (range) from the end of the runway as displayed on the controller's radarscope. The controller will provide recommended altitudes on final approach if requested by the pilot. (See PAR Approach) (Refer to AIM)

target symbol—A computer-generated indication shown on a radar display resulting from a primary radar return or a radar beacon reply.

taxi—The movement of an airplane under its own power on the surface of an airport (FAR Part 135.100—Note). Also, it describes the surface movement of helicopters equipped with wheels. (See Air Taxi, Hover Taxi) (Refer to AIM)

taxi into position and hold—Used by ATC to inform a pilot to taxi onto the departure runway in takeoff position and hold. It is not authorization for takeoff. It is used when takeoff clearance cannot immediately be issued because of traffic or other reasons. (See Hold, Cleared for Takeoff)

telephone information briefing service (TIBS)—A continuous telephone recording of meteorological and/or aeronautical information. (Refer to AIM)

terminal area facility—A facility providing air traffic control service for arriving and departing IFR, VFR, Special VFR, and on occasion en route aircraft. (See Approach Control, Tower)

terminal radar program—A national program instituted to extend the terminal radar services provided IFR aircraft to VFR aircraft. Pilot participation in the program is urged but is not mandatory. The program is divided into two parts and referred to as Stage II and Stage III. The Stage service provided at a particular location is contained in the Airport/Facility Directory.

- Stage I originally comprised two basic radar services (traffic advisories and limited vectoring to VFR aircraft). These services are provided by all commissioned terminal radar facilities, but the term "Stage I" has been deleted from use.
- Stage II/Radar Advisory and Sequencing for VFR Aircraft-Provides, in addition to the basic radar services, vectoring and sequencing on a full-time basis to arriving VFR aircraft. The purpose is to adjust the flow of arriving IFR and VFR aircraft into the traffic pattern in a safe and orderly manner and to provide traffic advisories to departing VFR aircraft.
- Stage III/Radar Sequencing and Separation Service for VFR Aircraft-Provides, in addition to the basic radar services and Stage II, separation between all participating VFR aircraft. The purpose is to provide separation between all participating VFR aircraft and all IFR aircraft operating within the airspace defined as a Terminal Radar Service Area (TRSA) or Terminal Control Area(TCA). (See Controlled Airspace, Terminal radar Service Area) (Refer to AIM, Airport/Facility Directory)

terminal radar service area/TRSA—Airspace surrounding designated airports wherein ATC provides radar vectoring, sequencing, and separation on a full-time basis for all IFR and participating VFR aircraft. Service provided in a TRSA is called Stage III Service. The AIM contains an explanation of TRSA. TRSA's are depicted on VFR aeronautical charts. Pilot participation is urged but is not mandatory. (See Terminal Radar Program) (Refer to AIM, Airport/Facility Directory)

threshold—The beginning of the portion of the runway usable for landing. (See Airport Lighting, Displaced Threshold)

touchdown zone—The first 3,000 feet of the runway beginning at the threshold. The area is used for determination of Touchdown Zone Elevation in the development of straight-in landing minimums for instrument approaches.

track—The actual flight path of an aircraft over the surface of the earth. (See Course, Route, Flight Path)

traffic advisories—Advisories issued to alert pilots to other known or observed air traffic which may be in such proximity to the position or intended route of flight of their aircraft to warrant their attention. Such advisories may be based on:

- Visual observation.
- Observation of radar identified and nonidentified aircraft targets on an ATC radar display, or
- Verbal reports from pilots or other facilities.

The word "traffic"followed by additional information, if known, is used to provide such advisories; e.g., "Traffic, 2 o'clock, one zero miles, southbound, eight thousand."

Traffic advisory service will be provided to the extent possible depending on higher priority duties of the controller or other limitations, e.g., radar limitations, volume of traffic, frequency congestion, or controller work load. Radar/nonradar traffic advisories do not relieve the pilot of his responsibility to see and avoid other aircraft. Pilots are cautioned that there are many times when the controller is not able to give traffic advisories concerning all traffic in the aircraft's proximity; in other words, when a pilot requests or is receiving traffic advisories, he should not assume that all traffic will be issued. (Refer to AIM, Radar Traffic Information Service)

traffic alert and collision avoidance system/TCAS—An airborne collision avoidance system based on radar beacon signals which operates independent of ground-based equipment. TCAS-I generates traffic advisories only. TCAS-II generates traffic advisories, and resolution (collision avoidance) advisories in the vertical plane.

traffic no longer a factor—Indicates that the traffic described in a previously issued traffic advisory is no longer a factor.

traffic pattern—The traffic flow that is prescribed for aircraft landing at, taxiing on, or taking off from an airport. The components of a typical traffic pattern are upwind leg, crosswind leg, downwind leg, base leg, and final approach.

- Upwind Leg—A flight path parallel to the landing runway in the direction of landing.
- Crosswind leg—A flight path at right angles to the landing runway off its upwind end.

- Downwind Leg—A flight path parallel to the landing runway in the direction opposite to landing. The downwind leg normally extends between the crosswind leg and the base leg.
- Base Leg—A flight path at right angles to the landing runway off its approach end. The base leg normally extends from the downwind leg to the intersection of the extended runway centerline.
- Final Approach—A flight path in the direction of landing along the extended runway centerline. The final approach normally extends from the base leg to the runway. An aircraft making straight-in approach VFR is also considered to be on final approach. (See Straight-In Approach- VFR, Taxi Patterns) (Refer to AIM, FAR Part 91)

transponder—The airborne radar beacon receiver/transmitter portion of the Air Traffic Control Radar Beacon System (ATCRBS) which automatically receives radio signals from interrogators on the ground, and selectively replies with a specific reply pulse or pulse group only to those interrogations being received on the mode to which it is set to respond. (See Interrogator) (Refer to AIM)

ultralight vehicle—An aeronautical vehicle operated for sport or recreational purposes which does not require FAA registration, an airworthiness certificate, nor pilot certification. They are primarily single occupant vehicles, although some two-place vehicles are authorized for training purposes. Operation of an ultralight vehicle in certain airspace requires authorization from ATC. (See FAR 103)

uncontrolled airspace—Uncontrolled airspace is that portion of the airspace that has not been designated as continental control area, control area, control zone, terminal control area, or transition area and within which ATC has neither the authority nor the responsibility for exercising control over air traffic. (See Controlled Airspace)

unicom—A nongovernment communication facility which may provide airport information at certain airports. Locations and frequencies of UNICOMs are shown on aeronautical charts and publications. (Refer to AIM, Airport/Facility Directory)

unpublished route—A route for which no minimum altitude is published or charted for pilot use. It may include a direct route between NAVAIDS, a radial, a radar vector, or a final approach course beyond the segments of an instrument approach procedure. (See Published Route, Route)

very high frequency/VHF—The frequency band between 30 and 300 mHz. Portions of this band, 108 to 118 mHz, are used for certain navaids; 118 to 136 mHz are used for civil air/ground voice communications. Other frequencies in this band are used for purposes not related to air traffic control.

VFR conditions—Weather conditions equal to or better than the minimum for flight under visual flight rules. The term may be used as an ATC clearance/instruction only when:

- An IFR aircraft requests a climb/descent in VFR conditions.
- The clearance will result in noise abatement benefits where part of the IFR departure route does not conform to an FAA approved noise abatement route or altitude.
- A pilot has requested a practice instrument approach and is not on an IFR flight plan.

All pilots receiving this authorization must comply with the VFR visibility and distance from cloud criteria in FAR Part 91. Use of the term does not relieve controllers of their responsibility to separate aircraft in TCAs/TRSAs as required by FAA Handbook 7110.65. When used as an ATC clearance/instruction, the term may be abbreviated.

VFR-on-top—ATC authorization for an IFR aircraft to operate in VFR conditions at any appropriate VFR altitude (as specified in FAR and as restricted by ATC). A pilot receiving this authorization must comply with the VFR visibility, distance from cloud criteria, and the minimum IFR altitudes specified in FAR Part 91. The use of this term does not relieve controllers of their responsibility to separate aircraft in TCAs/TRSAs as required by FAA Handbook 7110.65.

VFR not recommended—An advisory provided by flight service station to a pilot during a preflight or in-flight weather briefing that flight under visual flight rules is not recommended. To be given when the current and/or forecast weather conditions are at or below VFR minimums. It does not abrogate the pilot's authority to make his own decision.

visual approach—An approach wherein an aircraft on an IFR flight plan, operating in VFR conditions under the control of an air traffic control facility and having an air traffic control authorization, may proceed to the airport of destination in VFR conditions.

visual flight rules/VFR—Rules that govern the procedures for conducting flight under visual conditions. The term "VFR" is also used in the

United States to indicate weather conditions that are equal to or greater than minimum VFR requirements. In addition, it is used by pilots and controllers to indicate type of flight plan. (See Instrument Flight Rules, Instrument Meteorological Condition, Visual Meteorological Conditions) (Refer to FAR, Part 91 and AIM)

visual holding—The holding of aircraft at selected, prominent geographical fixes which can be easily recognized from the air. (See Hold, Holding Fixes)

visual meteorological conditions/VMC—Meteorological conditions expressed in terms of visibility, distance from cloud, and ceiling equal to or better than specified minima. (See Instrument Flight Rules, Instrument Meteorological Conditions, Visual Flight Rules)

visual separation—A means employed by ATC to separate aircraft in terminal areas. There are two ways to effect this separation:

- The tower controller sees the aircraft involved and issues instructions, as necessary, to ensure that the aircraft avoid each other.
- A pilot sees the other aircraft involved and upon instructions from the controller provides his own separation by maneuvering his aircraft as necessary to avoid it. This may involve following another aircraft or keeping it in sight until it is no longer a factor. (See See and Avoid) Refer to FAR, Part 91)

vortices/wing tip vortices—Circular patterns of air created by the movement of an airfoil through the air when generating lift. As an airfoil moves through the atmosphere in sustained flight, an area of low pressure is created above it. The air flowing from the high pressure area to the low pressure area around and about the tips of the airfoil tends to roll up into two rapidly rotating vortices, cylindrical in shape. These vortices are the most predominant parts of aircraft wake turbulence and their rotational force is dependent upon the wing loading, gross weight, and speed of the generating aircraft. The vortices from medium to heavy aircraft can be of extremely high velocity and hazardous to smaller aircraft. (See Aircraft Classes Wake Turbulence) (Refer to AIM)

VOR/very high frequency omnidirectional range station—A ground-based electronic navigation aid transmitting very high frequency navigation signals, 360° in azimuth, oriented from magnetic north. Used as the basis for navigation in the National Airspace System. The VOR periodically identifies itself by Morse Code and may have an additional voice identification feature. Voice features may be used by ATC or FSS for transmitting instructions/information to pilots. (See Navigational Aid) (Refer to AIM)

wake turbulence—Phenomena resulting from the passage of an aircraft through the atmosphere. The term includes vortices, thrust stream turbulence, jet blast, jet wash, propeller wash, and rotor wash both on the ground and in the air. (See Aircraft Classes, Jet Blast, Vortices) (Refer to AIM)

wilco—I have received your message, understand it, and will comply with it.

Index

Other Bestsellers of Related Interest

GOOD TAKEOFFS AND GOOD LANDINGS—Joe Christy

This book is a reference that thoroughly examines takeoffs and landings, and the critical transitions accompanying each, for single-engine aircraft. The author stresses that every pilot must continually evaluate ever-changing factors of wind, air pressure, precipitation, traffic, temperature, visibility, runway length, and braking conditions. *Good Takeoffs and Good Landings* belongs on every pilot's required reading list. 192 pages, 70 illustrations. Book No. 2487, $14.95 paperback, $21.95 hardcover

from the TAB Practical Flying Series . . .
THE PILOT'S RADIO COMMUNICATIONS HANDBOOK—3rd Edition—Paul E. Illman and Jay Pouzar

". . . should have a spot on your bookshelf. . ."—Private Pilot

". . . time spent on this book is sure to make your flight smoother." —Kitplanes

An updated edition of a popular handbook. Contains new information on FAA rule changes regarding Mode C transponders, single-class TCA operations, and student pilot TCA training requirements. Current issues relating to the entire spectrum of VFR radio communications are addressed. This guide will help you use even the busiest airports with confidence and skill. 240 pages, 61 illustrations. Book No. 2445, $15.95 paperback only

THE BEGINNER'S GUIDE TO FLIGHT INSTRUCTION—2nd Edition—John L. Nelson

Get the best value for your flying dollars! This guide provides up-to-date information on training requirements, costs of flight instruction, career possibilities, pilot responsibilities, and more. Covers how to choose a training program, how much it will cost, and what to expect from the flight exam. 208 pages, Illustrated. Book No. 2443, $12.95 paperback only

YOUR PILOT'S LICENSE—4th Edition—Joe Christy

Completely revised, this book offers all the information on student training requirements, flight procedures, and air regulations. It tells you what the physical qualifications are, frankly discusses the expense involved, explains the integral role ground study plays in learning to fly, and even supplies a sample written test comparable to the actual Private Pilot's Written Test. Active pilots and flight instructors will find this an excellent refresher reference, too! 176 pages, 73 illustrations. Book No. 2477, $12.95 paperback only

OCEAN FLYING—2nd Edition—Louise Sacchi

A solidly authoritative volume that provides practical guidance on every aspect of ocean flying in general aviation aircraft. Valuable, tested-in-action information is presented on preflight and preparation, engine care and feeding, using charts efficiently, using the magnetic compass, weather interpretation, and more. 230 pages, Illustrated. Book No. 2436, $16.95 paperback, $24.95 hardcover

AVOIDING COMMON PILOT ERRORS—A Traffic Controller's View—John Stewart

A pilot, flight instructor, and air traffic controller of 20 years' experience cites examples of recurring pilot error. Improper training, lack of preflight preparation, poor communication skills, and confusing regulations are among the problems discussed. 240 pages, Illustrated. Book No. 2434, $16.95 paperback, $25.95 hardcover

---

Look for These and Other TAB Books at Your Local BOOKSTORE

To Order Call Toll Free 1-800-822-8158
(in PA and AK call 717-794-2191)

or write to TAB BOOKS Inc., Blue Ridge Summit, PA 17294-0840.

For a catalog describing more than 1300 titles, write to TAB BOOKS Inc., Blue Ridge Summit, PA 17294-0840. Catalog is free with purchase; otherwise send $1.00 in check or money order made payable to TAB BOOKS Inc. (and receive $1.00 credit on your next purchase).

CROSS-COUNTRY FLYING—2nd Edition—Paul Garrison, revised by Norval Kennedy

The first edition of *Cross-Country Flying* has become the standard guide in its field. Now, this classic sourcebook is available in an expanded, revised, and updated new edition. Whether you're a seasoned, intermediate, or student pilot, this new version will serve as an ideal base line for you to establish your own safe flying habits. Filled with solid advice that no student-pilot program can match, it's a volume that every pilot will want as a permanent cockpit companion. 208 pages, 101 illustrations. Book No. 2406, $13.95 paperback, $22.95 hardcover

MOVING THROUGH THE RATINGS: Passing From Private to Professional—Warren and Vici DeHaan

Now, a guide spells out just exactly what it takes to prepare for a career as an aviation professional. Here is all the information you need to map your progress as you move through the ratings from first-day student pilot to airline captain! A listing of colleges and universities with recognized aviation programs is highlighted in this outstanding selection. 224 pages, 49 illustrations. Book No. 2400, $15.95 paperback, $21.95 hardcover

. . . from the TAB Practical Flying Series
MASTERING INSTRUMENT FLYING—Henry Sollman with Sherwood Harris

Mastering Instrument Flying introduces an entirely new course designed from beginning to end to meet or exceed the Instrument Flight Test standards recently published by the FAA. The elements, techniques, procedures, and tolerances of instrument flight are addressed in precise detail. Fully illustrated information on how to prepare for the instrument flight test is provided, and additional advanced procedures not specifically required for the instrument rating are covered. 336 pages, 256 illustrations. Book No. 2433, $16.95 paperback, $24.95 hardcover

I LEARNED ABOUT FLYING FROM THAT—Editors of *FLYING*® Magazine

The editors of *FLYING* Magazine have selected the very best from their publication's most popular regular feature to come up with a series of sometimes humorous, always candid, flying stories. These exciting tales by dozens of high-time pilots—including airman-aerobat Paul Mantz, pilot-author Richard Bach, movie stunt pilots, and many others—all provide valuable flying lessons! 322 pages, 8 illustrations. Book No. 2393, $14.95 paperback only